THE EFFETE CONSPIRACY

The Effete Conspiracy

#

ALSO BY BEN H. BAGDIKIAN

In the Midst of Plenty: The Poor in America

The Information Machines: Their Impact on Men and the Media

AND OTHER CRIMES BY THE PRESS

Ben H. Bagdikian

Harper & Row, Publishers

NEW YORK, EVANSTON
SAN FRANCISCO
LONDON

1817

Chapters cited below originally appeared, in somewhat different form, in the following:

"What's Wrong with the American Press" in the March 1967 issue of *Esquire* under the title "The American Newspaper Is Neither Record, Mirror, Journal, Ledger, Bulletin, Telegram, Examiner, Register, Chronicle, Gazette, Observer, Monitor, Transcript Nor Herald of the Days Events"

"Meddling with the Government: Lessons of the Pentagon Papers" in the September/October 1971 issue of the *Columbia Journalism Review* under the title "What Did We Learn"

"PR Infiltrates the Press" in the Fall 1963 issue of the *Columbia Journalism Review* under the title "Journalist Meets Propagandist"

"The Gentle Suppression" in the Spring 1965 issue of the *Columbia Journalism Review*

"Alas, the Small-Town Press" in the December 1964 issue of *Harper's Magazine* under the title "Behold the Grassroots Press, Alas!"

"News as a Byproduct" in the Spring 1967 issue of the *Columbia Journalism Review*

"The 'Independent' Newspapers of the Du Ponts" in the Spring 1964 issue of the *Columbia Journalism Review* under the title "Case History: Wilmington's 'Independent' Newspapers"

"Houston Listens to the Ghost of Jesse Jones" in the August 1966 issue of *The Atlantic Monthly* under the title "Houston's Shackled Press"

(Continued)

STANDARD BOOK NUMBER: 06-010179-2

LIBRARY OF CONGRESS CATALOG CARD NUMBER: 70-184371

"Television, the President's Medium" in the Summer 1962 issue of the *Columbia Journalism Review*

"From JFK to LBJ: From Cool to Hot" in the Winter 1964 issue of the *Columbia Journalism Review* under the title "JFK to LBJ: Paradoxes of Change"

"The Camp in the Congo; or, Why It Is That What the President Reads in the *Post* and the *Times* Spoils Other People's Breakfasts" in the Fall 1962 issue of the *Columbia Journalism Review* under the title "The Morning Line"

"When the President Unspeaks" in the Spring 1963 issue of the *Columbia Journalism Review* under the title "The President Nonspeaks"

"LBJ and the Press; or, The Commander-in-Chief Thought He Was Editor-in-Chief" in the Winter 1965 issue of the *Columbia Journalism Review* under the title "The Era of Johnsonian Normalcy"

"The President Just Another Flack?" in the Summer 1965 issue of the *Columbia Journalism Review* under the title "Press Agent—But Still President"

"The Great Nixon-Agnew Media Con Game; or, A Few Plain Facts About the Politics of Newspapers" in the March/April 1971 issue of the *Columbia Journalism Review*

To
B. L. M.

Contents

#

III. The President and the Press

WITHDRAWN

Acknowledgments

―――――
#

Many of these essays are possible because reporters were willing to talk about their problems and their mistakes. A few proprietors did the same.

Research on the politics of the press in the use of columnists was done with assistance from Nan Robinson. I am also grateful to Jan Wentworth for work on the politics of the Ninety-first Congress as related to the politics of newspapers.

Introduction

#

What Sigmund Freud did for sex, Spiro Agnew has done for the American newspaper publisher. The Vice-President has found a way to relieve the owners of daily papers of microscopic guilt over their conservative bias.

Freud explained various human hang-ups by traumas in early life which led to reversion to infantile sexuality and Oedipus complexes. Newspaper publishers are peculiarly vulnerable to analogous complaints. Early in every publisher's career there comes a traumatic moment when he realizes that most of the reporters he is paying seem to be Democrats, which for a Republican publisher is like a man discovering that his son likes boys better than girls. This throws the publisher into a state of ideological panic, with regression to infantile economics and politics of such a primitive kind that his editorials thereafter embarrass his conservative idols such as Milton Friedman and Arthur Burns. He develops weird oedipal feelings about the relationship of his newspaper to the government, producing a beautiful love-hate syndrome. On the one hand he wants the mother government to practice passionate socialism with the corporate side of his paper, granting lavish subsidies in postal rates, exemptions from antitrust laws, avoidance of child labor laws and other loving gifts. But at the same time his paper uses its editorial page to demand absolute free enterprise for its readers in such matters as welfare and medicine, with incantations against "big government" and "the welfare state."

Nevertheless, the poor fellows have moments of guilt and contrition. They used to keep reporters out of the crucial sessions of the American Newspaper Publishers Association and finally let their employees in, thus confirming for the reporters that it was all pretty boring. Occasionally the publishers took their culture in their hands and asked long-haired youths to address them at their conventions. Now and then a more enterprising entrepreneur would wonder out loud why it was newspapers weren't keeping the best talent.

But Dr. Agnew ended this tension. He seemed to be saying: Relax, stop feeling guilty, you are wronged by your staffs. It is perfectly normal, in fact good, for a newspaper to be conservatively biased, because that isn't bias at all, only true-blue Americanism, and you know it. You must not be distracted by a few deviants among you, like the *Washington Post* and the *New York Times,* for they are suffering from acute effetism; they are sick and a threat to society. Dick and I revere freedom of the press and it is with sadness that we occasionally find it necessary to sign committal papers to deliver such deviants for treatment in the local Federal District Court. Do not be ashamed of forcing your staffs to show proper regard for Our Leaders. Remember that they are wayward children and probably hated their fathers and are ashamed of their education and affluence.

So the American press has been worrying for the last few years about its alleged liberalism. Unfortunately, this has obscured another problem: the American daily press is conservative.

One of the essays in this book describes just how conservative and anachronistic the daily press is. Other chapters are concerned with misbehavior by various portions of the press. Some were written a few years ago and it occurred to me that perhaps things had changed. The *Houston Chronicle,* for example, like many papers, is run by the city's ruling oligarchy, with its news and editorial policies designed to fit the owners' other financial and political interests. It is so wedded to this doctrine that it fired a successful editor because the editor discovered, among other things, that 30 percent of the city was black, something whites would never have known by reading their leading paper. Has the *Chronicle* changed? Apparently not. In late 1971 they fired their religion reporter, Janice Law, because a story she wrote

offended a local Catholic hierarch who happened to be a friend of
her editor. The paper printed a retraction based on the statement of
the hierarch. The same day a document from the Vatican confirmed
that Mrs. Law's story had been correct and the editor's friend incorrect. But Mrs. Law remained fired, as was a second reporter
ordered to take Mrs. Law's place who then declined, having seen the
unbiased journalism required.

Another essay in the book describes how the Du Ponts of Delaware
ran their newspapers in about the same way. They, too, fired an
editor who thought that news should ignore the private interests of
the owners. Toward the end of 1971 Ralph Nader and his group
looked at the Du Pont empire, including its newspapers, and found
things depressingly unchanged.

Many of these essays have to do with the problems of government
and the press and with the failures of professional journalists. Journalists need constant criticism because they serve a crucial public
function in ways that are unavoidably subjective. The same is true of
their employers. As long as owners of newspapers remain out of
touch with their constituents and accept precepts of journalism that
are invalid, criticism of their employees remains secondary. Corporate
policymaking in newspapers has shaped news policy. How else could
so many decades have gone by without community newspapers looking critically at the business practices in their cities, at car dealers, at
tobacco-and-health, at medicines-and-health. These are all business
clients and associates and they were not treated by newspapers the
way less powerful people were treated. Newspapers for decades have
concentrated on "welfare cheaters" and burglars, while ignoring commercial enterprises that killed people with unsafe medicines and unsafe automobiles, or cheated consumers of billions of dollars with
price fixing and manipulation of regulatory agencies. The racial caste
system and poverty have existed in an affluent society dedicated to
equality and social justice partly because newspapers and broadcasters have had built-in biases over what is news and what is
important. For years newspapers have rejected staff members who
wanted to report on such severe social pathologies. Race and poverty
become news only when they become violent.

Criticism of individual journalists, nevertheless, should never end.
We are not without sin and sloth, and the errors of our employers are

no excuse for personal incompetence or unfairness. But concentrating solely on the work of the individual journalist while ignoring the flaws in the institution he works in is like watching an airliner lose its engines while the crew spends all its time fussing with the coffee-maker.

The external problems of the press and of broadcasters are not small. Government is big and increasingly willing to coerce the news media. And the audience is more and more fragmented, with fearful traditionalists at one end and innovative young people at the other. Universal communications have introduced the American people to alternative styles of life and these have produced bitter stresses. For society this means an impulse to self-destruction through punishing innovation. It also means that it is difficult under the best of conditions for the media to sense their public and speak to it. If the newspapers and broadcasters do what Nixon and Agnew want them to do, they will continue to emanate the values of the middle classes of the 1950s, which is the Nixonian ethic. As a result they will find themselves a few years from now speaking to a shrinking group of aging citizens resting their close-cropped hair on faded antimacassars.

True revolutionaries believe that the worse things get, the better, since only massively bad conditions will cause enough people to rise up and overthrow their government. In this view, serious reform and liberalism are the enemy. On this the Nixon-Agnew people and the revolutionaries agree, though for different reasons. The fact is that most newspapers and broadcasting stations also agree with Nixon-Agnew. If the mildly reformist *Post* and *Times* can be isolated or silenced, the progression toward total insignificance of the media will be complete. Newspapers will be heading toward a crash on the hillsides of change but they will have very good coffee on the way down.

I

SECRECY

AND MANIPULATION

···

1   What's Wrong with
the American Press

\#

This is a love story and like most love stories it begins with a touch of sadness and egoism. I love newspapers. I was a teen-age dirty old man with indiscriminate lust for every newspaper in sight. I made indecent advances in public places to any paper that came along, whether it was the *Boston Daily Record,* Hearst's hip-swinging little hooker, or the *Boston Transcript,* a little old lady in high choker collar. It sounds depraved but confidential studies show that this is a common adolescent experience and society must stop imposing feelings of shame. Besides, I grew up in a suburb of Boston whence came more bad newspapers than most cities and I read them with the same feverish appetite that I lavished on the copy of Spicy Adventure Stories hidden under the cellar stairs.

I can remember the day I stopped looking at newspapers as mere love objects and began looking for their individual qualities. My father was a clergyman addicted to nonalcoholic beverages and the *Boston Traveler.* It was a sheltered childhood and I was sixteen before I realized that there are possibilities beyond sarsaparilla and sedative journalism. I had grown up on fearless editorials congratulating retiring battalion chiefs who had completed forty years of service to the Boston Fire Department without falling off a ladder.

Then one day, at a time when I was thinking of going to college, I read a *Traveler* editorial about a Dartmouth College dormitory fire that killed some students. The parents could take comfort, the editorial said, because it was a worrisome world we lived in and the dead students were spared further contact with it.

In the movies of that day, when the hero discovered his loved one in the arms of another man the background music came to a full stop. His eyes would widen to the size of jumbo olives. She would inhale like a helium balloon. And the orchestra would come back, *tutti,* with a tragic passage from Schubert's Eighth. I didn't have any background music when that editorial hit me in Stoneham, Massachusetts. But I did go to the window of my second-floor bedroom to look down at what it would be like to get back into the worrisome world in case of fire. I figured I could make it with a couple of broken ankles and I decided that newspapers weren't perfect.

I still love newspapers, but then I am a curable optimist. I was disillusioned some time ago about the hope that the average paper would enter the contemporary social and political world. Since the 1930s they had been pushing economics that Adam Smith rejected and the American electorate has steadily moved in the opposite direction. Editorial pages became sociological museums that let their owners browse lovingly among their ideological antiques. News columns insisted on being expressed in language and ideas that bore minimal resemblance to what went on inside the heads of most people.

(Let me interrupt this love story with a request that the usual defenders of the American press please refrain from writing to me about the splendid achievements of the Pulitzer Prize winners. If you insist on writing, address yourself to the 90 percent plus of daily papers that most people have to live with.)

But newspapers have other problems—nice mechanical, non-ideological problems. In the factory part of the business, where the papers are manufactured, the industry has been dragged kicking and screaming into the nineteenth century. Owners complain endlessly that their production costs are driving them wild. So I assumed that they would like help in oozing into the twentieth century at no cost to themselves. This is where I heard Schubert's Eighth again.

In 1967 I started a study of how new technology would change the news business. Computers and cable and fancy electronic printing methods were beginning to have an impact. The study was undertaken at RAND, a nonprofit research corporation that agreed to do it without using government funds. Although RAND's chief client, the Air Force, seemed to regard the corporation's concern for the problems of cities as an unacceptable diversion, RAND had not earned a reputation as an antiestablishment agitator. The idea was to get the big foundations to support the work, and if they did, the study could produce detailed information that would tell publishers of various sizes how much it would cost them to shift to the new machines during the coming years. Since this kind of support would be enhanced by cooperation from the publishing world, I spent time on correspondence and conferences with Stanford Smith, the general manager of the American Newspaper Publishers Association, which is to American journalism what the National Conference of Catholic Bishops is to American Catholicism.

After a chance meeting with me in Los Angeles, Mr. Smith talked to his good friend the ANPA president, J. Howard Wood, of the *Chicago Tribune*. A week later there appeared at my office in Santa Monica the West Coast correspondent of the *Chicago Tribune*, armed with a typed list of hostile questions. The poor fellow had the same pained expression on his face that I had seen on members of the police department bomb squad looking at an odd-shaped package in the bus station. The correspondent had with him a transcript of my testimony before the Senate Anti-Monopoly Subcommittee in which I had opposed special privileges for newspapers, in this case exemption from antitrust laws. Stanford Smith had testified in favor of the exemption. And of course, a few days later there was a hostile story in the *Chicago Tribune* about my study, mentioning in the second paragraph that some people in the study had been critical of newspapers in the past, and in the fourth paragraph that I had testified against the antitrust exemption for newspapers (as had a number of prominent publishers who are members of the ANPA).

Immediately thereafter, with a charming air of surprise, Mr. Smith sent a confidential ("for your information") memo to the members of the ANPA board of directors and its public relations committee: "The attached story in the *Chicago Tribune* of October

6 is the first I have seen bringing to public attention the fact that all
except one of the leaders of the Rand Corporation's study of the
newspaper business are highly active critics of newspapers. . . ." Mr.
Smith advised his members not to cooperate. He wrote: ". . . it is
just as wrong to appoint super-critics to run a study of the press as it
would be to appoint men who think that everything the press does
is right."

There appeared a couple of weeks later in the *Mexico* (Missouri)
Ledger, a paper run by an ANPA officer, an editorial condemning the
RAND study, a subject that presumably had been keeping the good
citizens of Mexico awake nights. And the editorial contained this
original phrase: "It is just as wrong to hire professional critics for a
study of the press, as it would be . . ."

A book did get published on the subject but a mass of detailed
economic studies of potential benefit to publishers remains in the
files, thanks to the reflex paranoia of the industry.

Newspapers today continue to stumble into the future, though at
the moment they are stumbling all the way to the bank.

Considering the great new market for news and the reaction of
most papers, the most kindly comment about contemporary American newspaper proprietors can be borrowed from a panhandler who
used to hang around Piccadilly Circus behind dark glasses, holding
a tin cup and a semiscrupulous sign that read: "Nearly Blind."

The newspaper trade literature is a litany of complaints about
rising costs, but the industry makes profits 76 percent higher than
the average for all American industries. Publishers have a standardized outrage at their obstinate unions, but most newspaper operators don't know enough about their own economics to realize where
their long-range self-interest lies. There are real problems for the
metropolitan papers confronted with sprawling suburbs, yet it was
only recently that a few brighter publishers perceived the uses of
scientific analysis to solve their technical problems. Dailies will
remain free and creative not as printing industries but as social institutions with a commanding purpose, like the local college, art museum
or bawdy house, yet most of them organize their corporations no
differently than textile mills.

The unique strength of the American daily is its roots in its own
community, yet indifferent and narrow local leadership of papers has

encouraged galloping consolidations so rapidly in the last ten years that by now most dailies are controlled by chains.

In their slow response to rising popular standards, publishers seem haunted by H. L. Mencken's aphorism "No one ever went broke underestimating the taste of the American public."

Mencken was wrong. Since World War II a lot of papers have gone broke that way, among them the *Boston Post,* the *Los Angeles Mirror,* the *Houston Press,* the *St. Petersburg Independent* the *New York World-Telegram,* the *New York Journal-American,* and most of the other petrified specimens in the old Hearst empire.

Mencken's own paper, the *Baltimore Sun,* has been a cornucopia of profits because it provided thorough national reporting, though it only recently woke up to its own community. The *New York Times* is the most solid property in that journalistically unhappy city for about the same reason with the same exception. The *Los Angeles Times* has turned handsome profits since it ended its career as a strident family trumpet and began being a good newspaper. The *Louisville Courier-Journal,* a high-quality paper in a small city in a poor state, has a balance sheet to gladden the heart of the Internal Revenue Service. The *Washington Post* made so much money that its late proprietor, Philip Graham, used to tell people he bought the stock of *Newsweek* magazine just to get rid of the profits jamming the *Post*'s cash register.

The source of the profits is obvious: the country is rich, it is reading and it is interested in public affairs.

The source of underlying trouble with newspapers is almost as obvious: most of them are riding this easy tide, complacent in their monopoly status, without making basic reforms that they and the readers deserve.

Some of the needed changes are relatively simple. Newspaper technology needs to be brought up to date, using science, engineering and rational problem-solving in mechanical and distribution problems. This requires a top-level, industry-wide working relationship with the craft unions.

The most fundamental reform is not so easy. Leadership and policy control on newspapers need to be made more responsive to the society at large, not as a mirror image of the body politic, but sensitive to social and economic reality as a good university is to learning.

Yet there is no organizational mechanism in newspapers to keep leadership responsive, as there is in higher education and in other large social enterprises, such as the better foundations and private agencies.

The problem has peculiar agonies for the newspaper because it has to be a godless corporation run for profit and at the same time a community institution operated for the public good, with the two functions largely insulated from each other. This requires the good publisher to have the mixed qualities of John Jacob Astor and Albert Schweitzer, a combination that would try the ingenuity of the most conscientious board of directors. Yet this crucial national institution is run by a multitude of mostly parochial businessmen selected by worse-than-conventional corporate happenstance. Colleges and shoe factories select their leaders with more care than the process by which men come to operate daily papers.

The good papers today are run by strong individuals, almost never by a committee or by trustees or by absentee owners. Their papers mean more to these individuals than any other enterprise in the world and they are driven by the obsession that whatever important happens in the world must be told to the readers by their local paper and that paper alone.

Most American dailies fail this standard. A few are excellent, most are mediocre, and many are wretched. The quality of reporting and editing has increased markedly in the last generation but this is no contradiction of the fact that most newspapers are failing their present duty. The new urgency in local and national events, the faster reaction time of all social movement and the dramatic change in the nature of the American audience is widening the gap between the responsibilities of the press and its performance.

The newspaper audience today is unrecognizable from the one in the twenties. Since that time people with family incomes over $6,000 (in constant dollars) increased from 18 million to 90 million. Men and women voting for President went from 29 million to 71 million; white collar and skilled workers from 16 million to 42 million. Just since World War II the number of adults with better than eighth-grade educations rose from 29 million to 67 million.

Newspapers congratulate themselves for keeping up with the change in size of the adult population, and this is largely true. But in the last ten years book sales have doubled; the number of new books on social and economic subjects has increased more than six times.

Social change, which provides the most dramatic materials for newspapers—or should—has accelerated at dizzying speed. The amount of knowledge is said to double every twelve years. Political evolution, which used to take decades, is sometimes measured in months. Its personal impact is enhanced by instant communication. The involvement of men in social affairs and in the world at large is magnified; men who in childhood could travel no farther than from Kansas City to Chicago in eight hours now can go from Kansas City to Paris in the same amount of time. The enlarged concern with national and global news is obvious.

Less noticed, especially by foreign observers and most nonprofessional American ones, is the deep involvement of the reader in community news, which, contrary to the European tradition, is not a sign of provincialism. The United States lacks true national papers not primarily because of its vast geography but because, unlike any other modern country, it organizes some of its central institutions—schools, police power, property taxes, etc.—on a local basis, voted on by the local citizen. Increasingly the American citizen has children in the public schools and worries about them, owns his own house, drives his own car, fights over zoning and city hall. No national paper, magazine or broadcasting network can tell him what he wants to know about such things.

How have American newspapers responded?

Most of them still cover their local governments wretchedly. It is common to have the primary ruling body hold open meetings without personal press coverage. Over half the papers in state capitals get most of their statehouse coverage from sources outside their own staff, like wire services, outside papers or press releases. Some quality coverage has been outstanding, but a mass of indifferent local papers remain.

In the face of enormously increased interest in public affairs, newspapers have reduced their average space devoted to news. In 1940 the average American daily had twenty-seven pages. In 1965 it had fifty pages. Of the additional twenty-three pages, three went to "news" and twenty to advertising. But during that same period the reader lost more than three pages of live news. Type size was enlarged and white space used more liberally, to make papers more readable. There was a radical increase in the number and size of photographs used. Syndicated features ranging from comics to political columns took vastly more space. Some of these elements have advantages for the serious reader but because they and the ads have eaten into former news space, the result is a decrease in live news. One rule of thumb of some editors is that it is impossible to tell the news adequately without a minimum of forty columns of "hard news"—what is left after subtracting ads, features, specialized information and entertainment. In some large cities the readers get an average of twenty columns.

Yet the modern audience is a collection of specialists, each looking for comprehensive information in his field; they include the baseball fan with his insatiable appetite, the PTA leader, the zoning fighter, the man who owns stocks, the man who drives a car, the new political activists. Mostly they look elsewhere because their paper fails them. News magazines, for example, tend to sell more copies where the local paper has inadequate news. *Time* sells twice as many copies per capita in Boston, San Francisco and Manchester, New Hampshire, as it does in Louisville, Nashville and New York.

Since World War II, sales of newspapers per family have dropped 18 percent. There are more cities than ever and fewer papers. Community growth has become volatile as newspapers have become more ponderous. In 1910 there were 2,200 dailies published in 1,200 cities; 53 percent of all urban places had their own paper. Today less than a quarter of urban places have their own paper, mostly because there are many more cities, partly because the number of papers is down to 1,750. The lack of a local paper with its function of tying together urban populations has increased the lack of community identity in urban America.

In 1910 the majority of cities with papers had competing ones; today less than 3 percent have.

One reason the newspapers have moved slowly and adapted clumsily is that most of them blind themselves with paranoid secrecy. Basic statistics common to other industries are clutched jealously by individual papers. Of all major economic activity in the country, publishers probably have the least accurate picture of themselves. Accounting methods are archaic and variable. Advertising rates are a Byzantine morass so arcane that often both paper and advertiser have trouble figuring out how much is being paid for what kind of space. Drifting in a forgiving economy, papers survive this with profit, but when their environment changes they are uncomprehending and sometimes unviable.

This is a contributing cause of monopoly. "The old monopoly"—domination of one city by one newspaper management—is just about complete. There are fifteen cities left (out of 1,400 newspaper cities) with face-to-face competition, a morning paper against a morning paper or an evening against an evening. At last count forty-five papers with two managements had divided their spheres of influence, one taking the morning, the other the evening. Half of these forty-five are semi-married, operating jointly in such areas as printing and the selling of ads. The remainder of the 1,400 cities have one newspaper.

"The new monopoly" is that of "groups," a word evolved from the old-fashioned "chain," as "funeral director" is from "undertaker." A group, or chain, consists of a single management that controls papers in more than one city. They are growing like wildfire. Ten years ago chains controlled 491 papers, or a third of all dailies. Today a majority of the 1,750 dailies are operated by chains.

Papers in trouble, because their hierarchs are at each other's throats or living in Majorca, are candidates for the chains. This is the secret of Samuel Newhouse, who controls eighteen papers. He keeps dossiers on papers that are not well run or are torn by dissension; when the inevitable time of trouble comes, he makes his offer. Newhouse appears to be uninterested in the local editorial product; his purchase agreement usually keeps in office the same crew that allowed the paper to drift. He brings in essentially national-caliber credit, rational management, accounting, purchasing and marketing. By applying ordinary modern business methods, he makes money where others threw it away. Editorially his papers usually are neither better nor worse than before.

The primary danger of chains is not that their operators are evil but that absentee owners are bad for American papers. So is ordinary corporate management.

Chains increase absentee ownership. And they deepen the tendency for monolithic politics in an institution already suffering from severe ideological ossification. The largest chains in circulation include Chicago Tribune, Scripps-Howard, Hearst, Newhouse, Knight, Gannett and Ridder. In leadership and in editorial views they are something less than a representative spectrum of American thought and values.

They tend not only to present single editorial views on any national issue but also to enlarge their corporate size on political grounds. When the conservative *Chicago Tribune* bought the *Fort Lauderdale News* in Florida, it was in the spirit of political camaraderie. The chief executive of the *News*, R. H. Gore, said: "There isn't another newspaper organization with whom I would have entertained negotiations. . . . Our basic philosophy on government . . . for community progress and civic upbringing is almost identical." If that part of Florida expected ideological relief it was wrong.

In 1964 a controversy between the Du Pont ownership of one of its Delaware papers and the paper's executive editor provoked the question of whether it would be better to avoid embarrassment by having the Du Pont holding company, Christiana Securities, sell the paper. In an internal memorandum, editor-publisher Charles L. Reese, Jr., told Lammot Du Pont Copeland, president of the Du Pont Company, that one way out would be:

Outright sale to an outside newspaper organization whose political and economic views closely parallel those of the present ownership. There are a number of such organizations. To avoid having the papers fall into unfriendly hands through a second sale, the sales agreement should give Christiana or its successors the first opportunity to purchase the papers if they should be again put up for sale.

The Du Ponts did not sell their papers but the conflict continued, causing the executive editor, Creed Black, to quit in protest.

The chains will probably continue to grow. Eighty percent of all newspaper sales since the war have been to other newspapers. The Internal Revenue Service has a rule against "unreasonable" accumulation of corporate income without normal taxation, but the Tax Court has ruled that using accumulations of newspaper profits to buy more newspapers is a "reasonable need of the business."

The underlying causes for both the old and the new monopolies are mass production and mass consumption, which favor the big operator. The best hope of the reader is to keep pressure on existing monopolies not to bifurcate from sheer corporate guilt, but to be more responsive to the community. The history of newspapers in modern times is that survival tends to go to the paper most serious about news. The *Chicago Tribune* is the best nineteenth-century newspaper in America; it thrives because it has always been diligent about news, even eccentric news.

The *New York Times* and the *New York Herald Tribune* entered World War II with roughly the same circulation. When wartime newsprint restrictions went into force, each had to make a decision: with a fixed size of paper, would they give more space to the advertisers who were clamoring to buy, or to the readers who wanted war news? The *Herald Tribune* decided it would solidify its financial position by selling more ads. The *Times* made a good, gray decision to put its space into news. The late Orvil Dryfoos, the publisher of the *Times*, said he thought this was a crucial decision that sent the *Times* into the postwar era in an unassailable position and the *Trib* into a decline.

The Canadian press lord, Roy Thomson, insists that he is interested only in newspaper balance sheets. In Saint Petersburg, Florida, he controlled the *Independent*, a dispirited, ultraconservative segregationist sheet. His competition was Nelson Poynter's *Times*. Poynter broke all the hard-boiled rules of newspaperdom. Saint Petersburg is "God's Waiting Room," a city of elderly, retired white people, walking about with canes, jealous of their pensions, ready-made conservatives. Poynter is a liberal and he fills his paper with national news, economic graphs, investigative stories from courthouse and statehouse, plugs for the liberal Democratic ethic. He makes a great deal of money. Thomson lost a great deal of money and finally persuaded Poynter to let the *Independent* collapse into Poynter's reluctant arms. The *Chicago Tribune,* an ultraconservative paper, and the *Saint Petersburg Times,* a liberal one, both survived and prospered because they were serious about their news.

Obviously many papers frivolous or incompetent in handling news survive and make profits, but almost always in monopoly towns or places where they have a peaceful coexistence pact with a similar competitor. The *New York Daily News* seems to be an exception. That tabloid is the country's largest, with 2,036,000 daily circulation (Sunday: 3,100,000). It is in the Zam-Pow-Zowie school of journalism, full of sex, crime and high jinks. To casual eyes it looks hostile to serious news, regarding great national matters about the way a high-flying drinker regards Antabuse. But looks are deceiving. It hires relatively high-class talent and, like the *Chicago Tribune,* a corporate and ideological cousin, it is serious and talented about the news it does go after. It reached its peak serving the city with the greatest and most steady infusion of semiliterate newcomers, first from abroad and then from unlettered rural areas and Puerto Rico. And now that its audience, along with everyone else's, is getting more sophisticated, the *Daily News* is running into rougher times and is reexamining its circulation base and news product.

Cities that still have competition could be helped by enactment of a law proposed by the American Newspaper Guild: let a paper be put up for sale to the highest bidder before it is merged or commits suicide. Many a competing paper has died because it was comatose from malnutrition and managerial abuse, but the death certificate was signed "Rising costs, labor trouble, etc." If a paper can bring a fair price on the market, why not let it live?

While most newspapers merely extend the practices and the politics of other papers, and most of these are conservative, putting papers up for public sale might attract new and contemporaneous blood. The most stultifying intellectual element in the press of the last two generations has been editorial rigidity in ideology, except that most editorial-page philosophy has not been sufficiently developed to be called ideology. It has gone far beyond presidential endorsements, though these were impressive: since the New Deal and until the Johnson phenomenon of 1964, American dailies have given Democrats no more than 23 percent support. This is only one sign of the alienation of most papers from their audience. To this day John Maynard Keynes is a profane name in editorials, though it is impossible to discuss post-World War I economics without him (he is somewhat dated now and inadequate, but he is still an editorial swear word.) Editorial pages helped make the word "Washington" a symbol of corruption and waste. "Planning" of any kind by any governmental unit for any purpose used to be considered un-American until newspaper circulation trucks began to have trouble getting away from the downtown areas and the cause turned out to be that cities were choking for lack of planning. Newspapers are now swinging in favor of community planning. Editorials didn't influence elections, but they have established the popular vocabulary of political and social dialogue. It has been a pinched and sterile dialogue which has inhibited the country's ability to see itself clearly.

With editorial creativity as with news, ultimately the answer lies with owners. Perhaps they will change for dollars-and-cents reasons. News play is changing, partly in sluggish response to demands of the audience, but also because advertisers, ironically, want it. The advertisers don't like newsstand sales. They want the paper in the home where it can be spread out and shared with all members of the family. So now newspapers are pushing home delivery as never before. The jazzy headline with the hoked-up news was created to catch the passing eye. Home delivery makes that meaningless.

The newspapers have discovered their delivery system was non-existent, farmed out to indifferent dealers, or tied to the touching "little merchant" movement. The latter let children buy papers from publishers and sell them, not as employees, but as independent free enterprisers, giving them a taste of self-reliance, thrift and the beauties of being a businessman. It also relieved the paper of a great deal of bookkeeping, the child labor laws and any liability if the little merchant was hit by a truck while carrying his papers. The papers used endless promotional stories run as news to attract "little merchants," citing how many captains of industry and political leaders once were newsboys. They almost never mentioned the little merchants who turned out to be con men. Or the one who became a certified Socialist: Norman Thomas once delivered newspapers for a publisher named Warren Gamaliel Harding.

The heart of the business is the editorial staff. Trying to be a first-rate reporter on the average American newspaper is like trying to play Bach's *Saint Matthew Passion* on a ukulele: the instrument is too crude for the work, for the audience and for the performer. This is the primary reason newspapers are not getting the best journalistic talent. Only about 17 percent of journalism school graduates go to newspapers. William Galbraith, Jr., then with the University of North Carolina, looked up the journalism school graduates who had been rated the best of the year by the journalism society, Sigma Delta Chi, and found that ten years later, of thirty-five leading graduates, only seven were working for newspapers. Half of them had never worked for a paper after graduation. The median salary for all was $12,600; for the newspapermen $8,164.

The money problem is relatively easy to solve. The qualities of good reporters and editors are those most wanted by a wide range of communications, corporate and governmental agencies. To increase newspaper editorial salaries by 23 percent in a very short time is not impossible and would prove what antiunion publishers have been telling reporters for years: that they are professional men for whom it is undignified to bargain for more money. The "average medium city newspaper," according to *Editor & Publisher* of April 16, 1966, showed a net profit in 1965 before taxes of 23 percent. This paper's total editorial budget, salaries and overhead was $584,200. It could raise this 40 percent and still show a profit of 17 percent, a tolerable reward.

But the chief reason talented men don't go to newspapers, or leave them after they do, is that the work of most papers is psychically unrewarding. A study by Frederick Yu and Ray L. Sweigert at the Columbia Graduate School of Journalism shows that with 320 graduates of that school the chief reasons for wanting to enter journalism were to achieve personal fulfillment and accomplish some useful social purpose. The lack of substantial and serious work with intelligent leadership is the greatest single recruiting agent for the American Newspaper Guild, though most publishers learn slowly that their reporters most often join the union because they aren't worked hard enough.

Some of the demoralizing practices in newspaperdom range from idiocy to mere habit. Professor Scott Cutlip of the University of Wisconsin estimates that one-third of all newspaper "news" content is inspired by public relations agents, who of course are then relieved of having to buy advertisements. Small papers are filled with canned editorials and commercial and political plugs paid for by the beneficiary. Big papers have institutionalized payola in their use of fashion and food photographs (often expensive color plates), with paid-for junkets for their special editors. Some great metropolitan papers as well as many smaller ones run paid-for advertising as though it were news.

The Post Office Department could rectify this easily and, possibly, fine almost every publisher in the country. Title 39 of U.S. Code, Section 4367, reads: "Editorial or other reading matter contained in publications entered as second-class mail, and for the publication of which valuable consideration is paid, accepted or promised, shall be marked plainly *advertisement* by the publisher." Fine: $550.

The Post Office could help in a more basic move to bring papers close to their communities. Postal law requires papers using second-class privileges to publish names of stockholders and officers, which most papers do in early October in the smallest available type in the most obscure part of the paper. Most of the listings are meaningless, making no distinction between small and large stockholders and substituting corporate or trust agents for unnamed principals. Listing the beneficial owners with the extent of their holdings would at least identify who controls a city's news.

Another measure might be local press councils, suggested years ago by Barry Bingham, editor and owner of the *Louisville Courier-Journal,* in which the paper's top leadership would sit regularly with community representatives, not to have a town committee edit the paper but to establish some human relationship between audience and the news establishment.

The ending of financial and policy secrecy by newspaper managements might eliminate unwarranted cynicism by the public and act as therapy on managements that need the light of day on their internal affairs. The Securities and Exchange Commission requires various companies whose stock is traded to list all those who own more than 10 percent in the business, and it obliges each of these to indicate other significant holdings in other traded companies.

A brave owner someday will provide for a community ombudsman on his paper's board—maybe a nonvoting one—to be present, to speak, to provide a symbol and, with luck, to represent public interest in the ultimate fate of the American newspaper.

Disclosure of financial interests, a greater openness in policy-making, a place for public representation could do for newspapers what they did for the post-Crash Stock Exchange: restore public confidence in the men who stand behind pieces of paper.

2   Meddling with the Government:
Lessons of the Pentagon Papers

\#

To the casual eye, the newsroom of the *Washington Post* at mid-afternoon on June 30, 1971, must have looked normal—normal, that is, for the *Post*: cramped, noisy, anarchic-democratic—the most interesting journalistic slum in America. There were no obvious signs of stress created by nearly three weeks of the most extraordinary events in the history of American journalism.

At one end of the newsroom the *Post*'s owner and publisher, Katharine Graham, and its executive editor, Benjamin Bradlee, and a small band of associated sufferers were awaiting word from company lawyers at the Supreme Court Building, two miles away. In the middle of the newsroom, Mary Lou Beatty, deputy national editor, held an open telephone line to the Supreme Court pressroom, waiting for the paper's court reporters to be handed the printed decision. In a communications room, Eugene Patterson, then managing editor, monitored the wire machines in case the first word came from them. Suddenly Miss Beatty held up her hands as she listened to a court reporter at the other end of the line riffle through the fifty-six-page decision. She yelled toward the executives: "It looks as though we've won." Then Gene Patterson rushed out of the wire room, leaped onto a desk, and with his hands cupped around his mouth shouted: "We win, six to three!"

In the euphoria of the newsroom that afternoon and throughout the country's journalistic establishment in the weeks since, something ominous seems to have escaped notice. It is not the fact that the newspapers and journalists might be criminally prosecuted or cited for contempt when asked to testify about their sources—though at this writing there is a grand jury sitting and the government is emanating strong signals. The journalists are affluent and well known and will march to court with much public notice and skilled lawyers, and at worst will probably avoid the psychopathic horrors of contemporary prisons; it is the uncelebrated little people who get quietly locked up on dubious grounds without glory.

The euphoria is unjustified because the Supreme Court decision probably signalizes not the triumphant end but the start of a struggle. The astonishing cluster of major issues involved in the court case moves onward with an uncertain future: legitimacy of the war in Vietnam; deception by the government; secrecy in government; and freedom of the press.

This is not to slight the accomplishments so far. The *New York Times* acquired the Pentagon Papers first and took the icy plunge without benefit of precedent. Once the *Times* was silenced, the *Post* went ahead knowing that it would be hauled into court and knowing that the Nixon administration hates the *Post* and the *Times* with a passion deeper than Spiro Agnew's thesaurus. Other metropolitan papers followed the silencing of the *Post* and *Times* with their own slices of the secret papers. Like relics of Saint George, whose spine is in Portofino, his skull in Rome, a hand in Genoa, a finger in London, the bits and pieces of the Pentagon Papers had escaped their secret reliquary in the crypts of the government and reappeared throughout the country in a finally credible sense of reality about the government and the war and a metastasized affront to the Espionage Act. The major papers did not shirk their duty and the Supreme Court upheld them.

But the Supreme Court victory should not obscure some troublesome facts. Courts officially ordered American newspapers not to publish certain materials because these materials offended the government (like all censoring governments, Mr. Nixon's claimed that the offensive material would do grave and irreparable harm to the nation). From June 15 to June 30 there was official, effective, court-enforced suppression of information in the hands of American newspapers. Nothing prevents the government from bringing similar suits in the future, and win or not in the Supreme Court, it can suppress information for a period of time and intimidate a paper.

Government antagonism to the press is not new or bad. The press shouldn't expect to be loved. Franklin Roosevelt had a running battle with publishers; Harry Truman ridiculed "newspaper talk"; Dwight Eisenhower viewed the press with cool contempt; John Kennedy enjoyed periodic outbursts of venom on the subject; and Lyndon Johnson's sentiments about newspapers would cause Bella Abzug to blush. But this administration has a special attitude toward the working press that is ideological and cultural; it has a political stake in spreading hatred of the metropolitan press; and unlike other administrations that fought with the press, this one has an itch for the jugular.

A major reason given by some judges for refusing the government request was that Congress had not yet passed a law giving the President the power to censor the press. If such a law existed, these judges said, the decision might have been different. In 1917, in a time of war and hysteria about spying, Congress specifically voted down an amendment to the Espionage Act that would have made the President a censor. In 1950, during the height of McCarthyism, the Espionage Act was amended to say—with puzzling implications—that nothing in the act shall infringe on freedom of the press. Secrecy in government is by executive order, not law.

Given the Nixon administration approach to the free press and broadcasting, the tendency of this Court is not encouraging. Only three justices—Black, Douglas and Brennan—explicitly turned their backs on the idea of both presidential and congressional power to censor. Justice Black said that when he reads that the First Amendment says Congress shall make no law abridging freedom of the press, he interprets "no law to mean no law." To which Erwin Griswold, Solicitor General, representing the government, replied: "I can only say, Mr. Justice, that to me it is equally obvious that 'no law' does not mean 'no law.' . . . The First Amendment was not intended to make it impossible for the Executive to function or to protect the security of the United States." Each of the nine justices felt impelled to write a separate opinion, and if one reads these for attitudes on the legitimacy of Congress's taking up a measure to give the President censorship powers, the apparent willingness to accept this is six to three.

The reversed six to three is ironic, but so was much more in the case. The *New York Times*'s regular law firm, Lord, Day & Lord, did not take up the case. Its head is former Attorney General Herbert Brownell. The *Washington Post*'s law firm, Royall, Koegel & Wells, did take up the case. Its former head is the present Secretary of State and presumably one of the aggrieved parties in the printing of the Pentagon Papers, William P. Rogers. The case also saw those "strict constructionists" John Mitchell and Richard Nixon asking the Supreme Court to "make law"—that is, give the President powers that Congress had refused.

Some judges asked in all earnestness why a responsible newspaper would not ask the government what part of official papers it could publish. It is a discouraging question, asking that papers accept informally what the First Amendment forbids officially, putting a construction on "responsible" that makes the press an instrument of official policy on the most vital issues. This was not the kind of issue the framers of the Constitution had in mind. The First Amendment was not written with the idea that the press would be free to print the names of donors to the Santa Claus Fund but have to ask the government for permission to write about war and peace.

In addition, there seemed in some justices to be a personal hostility to the press. Chief Justice Burger wrote: "To me it is hardly believable that a newspaper long regarded as a great institution in American life would fail to perform one of the basic and simple duties of every citizen with respect to the discovery or possession of stolen property or secret government documents. That duty, I had thought—perhaps naïvely—was to report forthwith, to responsible public officers. This duty rests on taxi drivers, Justices, and the New York *Times*." He added in a footnote: "Interestingly, the *Times* explained its refusal to allow the Government to examine its own purloined documents by saying in substance this might compromise their sources and informants! The *Times* thus asserts a right to guard the secrecy of its sources while denying that the Government of the United States has that power."

Judge Blackmun exhibited the same feelings. He wrote: ". . . the Washington *Post*, on the excuse that it was trying to protect its source of information, initially refused to reveal what material it actually possessed. . . ." He concluded: "I strongly urge, and sincerely hope, that these two newspapers will be fully aware of their ultimate responsibility to the United States of America. . . ."

What emerged throughout the case was a dangerous naïveté among judges, lawyers and others about government propaganda, the frequency with which government agencies break the law or improperly invade privacy, and the true relationship between the federal government and the press in Washington. The grim and terrible condemnations about "secrets" look different when you know that highly placed government officials, beginning with the President of the United States and his cabinet, the Joint Chiefs of Staff and their staffs, regularly and systematically violate the Espionage Act—or at least the Attorney General's interpretation of it—by knowingly and deliberately disclosing secret information to the press.

The quantity of military secrets that appear in the press is directly related to appropriation hearings for the military services. If the Air Force wants a few billion dollars for a new weapons system, it leaks a few secrets that put the system in a good light. Two days later the Navy leaks other secrets about the same weapons system showing that it fails much of the time. Or the State Department, wanting to bluff another nation, lets out a secret that is a half-truth, then denies it the next day as "newspaper talk." And perhaps the Pentagon, which disapproved anyway, leaks the whole story of how the State Department leaked a half-truth. The net result is probably good because it is the only present remedy to secret government, but the point is that the U.S. government is the biggest player in town of the Leaking Secrets Game. Only when the secrets are embarrassing do the words "national security" come into play.

The idea that in matters of secrecy and responsibility the press is beholden to "the United States of America" sees the government as a policy monolith. There is no such entity, either in the Constitution or in practice. It is a pluralistic organism whose parts work on each other with various mechanisms, one of the more important being information. If the press did not obtain secrets or was not handed secrets on a silver platter, the government would have to invent some other way of getting out sequestered information.

The harm done by disclosure of secrets is minimal; the harm done by concealing information inside the secrecy system is enormous. President Kennedy ultimately told the *New York Times* that it should have printed more about the Bay of Pigs invasion of Cuba rather than less. Both the *Times* and the *Post* knew about the U-2 airplane flights over Russia months before the story broke. Both suppressed it in what they thought was the national interest. Soviet Russia knew about the plane all the time—its radar picked it up—but for a while it lacked planes and missiles with the range to shoot down the plane. Nonpublication merely kept the information from the Russian and American publics, a convenience to each government whose implications are interesting indeed. Ultimately the U-2 was shot down, with the result that lives were endangered, a summit conference was wrecked and a presidential visit to Moscow canceled—the usual scenario of what it is said will happen if secrets are published.

It seems safe to predict catastrophe if information is disclosed. If the information is protected by secrecy the prediction can never be tested, and keeping the secret seems the more prudent course. But intelligent, diligent men differ on the consequences of printing sensitive information. Justice White examined the government lists of "worst cases" it wanted suppressed in the Pentagon Papers and said he was confident that publication by the *Post* and *Times* "will do substantial damage to public interests." Justice Stewart looked at the same lists and said: "I cannot say that disclosure of any of them will surely result in direct, immediate, and irreparable damage to our nation or its people."

The judges were not the only ones who differed on the wisdom of publishing. There were arguments within the papers themselves. The *Post* reached its initial decision after about twelve continuous hours of intense debate. The argument, involving lawyers, editors, reporters and management, was fierce and prolonged. It ran through one deadline and was finally resolved five minutes before the deadline for the main edition. In the end, Katharine Graham took the full weight of argument and said yes.

As the lawyers and later the judges began looking beneath the awesome claim of TOP SECRET they began to see that it was seldom justified. List after list submitted by the government to the Court in secret was shown to be filled with items already in the public domain or already known to adversary nations. The government official brought in to testify in secret court session on how bad it would be to publish the documents later told Congress that at least six thousand pages of the seven thousand should not be classified.

Newspapermen in Washington already knew things like that. Last year during the heat of an armaments debate, the *Post* received in a plain envelope without return address a Xerox of a document marked SECRET—SENSITIVE. We called the Pentagon to confirm the document's authenticity and then printed it in full. It was a memorandum from Secretary of Defense Melvin Laird to his service secretaries and other military officials telling them they should say nothing in public that might imply that it would be good to have a moratorium on deploying MIRV missiles or ABMs. It was a directive to subordinates on what to say in public on an important public issue—a natural enough impulse from an official trying to win an argument among his rival officials in government. But SECRET? The *Post* received a letter from the Department of Defense telling it to turn over the memo under pain of prosecution under the Espionage Act.

When Mr. Laird was a member of the opposition in Congress, he wrote a stiff letter, in October 1966, demanding to know the government's negotiating position in the Vietnam war, including how many American troops we were offering to pull back in return for how many enemy troops. He demanded publicly that the government "should spell out clearly and unequivocally what our short-term aims and long-term objectives are with regard to South Vietnam and Southeast Asia." In 1966 Laird was goring the ox.

The issues involved are too profound to argue about whose ox is being gored, though that impels much of the secrecy machinery. What is more basic is that even when there is a discernible reason for keeping information secret, every piece of information marked SECRET erodes the basis for a free society. It excludes the citizen from the process of his own government, and that is a cost that has to be put into the "national security" equation.

This country was started on the assumption that legitimate government derives its powers from the consent of the governed, and if that means anything, those who are governed have to know what their government is doing. Yet we have lived under the spreading mystique of the official secret for so long that there is an assumption that information about public affairs is the private property of the government. Somewhere, somehow, the burden has shifted from the government's having to prove why it should conceal information, to the citizen, who now has to prove why he should be told. The Solicitor General even argued the analogy of the copyright law to the Supreme Court.

The country seems to have lost sight of the fact that true security lies in knowledge, not secrecy. During the Supreme Court hearing Justice Stewart asked the *Times*'s lawyer, Alexander Bickel, whether he would change his insistence on the constitutional right to publish if doing so would result in the death of "100 young men whose only offense had been that they were nineteen years old and had low draft numbers."

The information in the Pentagon Papers covers the years 1945–1968. The documents were not published during that period. More than one million Indochinese have been killed, more than fifty thousand young Americans were killed, we have spent $120 billion and have descended into one of the most poisonous eras in our time. The calculation of the costs of secrecy is not small.

The need for press freedom is not simply an intellectually elegant idea. The perfect secret is useless because information is powerful only if it causes men to understand their environment better. If information is secret, not enough people know enough to put the information to use, or to correct errors. The open society avoids catastrophic accumulations of maladjustment because everyone in the system is free to express himself and be heard by those who can make adjustments. "Responsibility" is not a safe standard. What is irresponsible to one man is responsible to another, or at another time. When Richard Nixon was a member of Congress he and his friends were prepared to send men to jail for suggesting normalizing relations with the Communist government of mainland China. It was a "bad," "treasonable," "subversive" idea. President Richard Nixon made a deliberate trip to China in order to start normalizing relations with the Communist government of mainland China.

The free marketplace of ideas, and the press's role in it, is not a luxury, nor is it a sometime thing to be tolerated only when it pleases the authorities. The press itself needs to remember its obligations. When the press insists on making its own decisions on publishing official information independent of government, it is sometimes painted as arrogant. But the reverse is true. For a newspaper to know something to be accurate and important and not to trust the public with it is arrogant. To withhold the truth from the public is to hold the public in contempt.

Justice Burger was amazed that the press would not give up its documents while criticizing government secrecy. Justice Blackmun thought that the *Post* was using protection of its sources as an "excuse." The fact is that government has the full force of its police powers to shut off the porosity of information that saves the United States government from the sickness of secrecy.

The anger of government at press intrusion is an ancient emotion. Roger L'Estrange was Licenser of the Press in London in 1680. He said: "A newspaper makes the multitude too familiar with the actions and councils of their superiors and gives them not only an itch but a kind of colorable right and license to be meddling with the government."

Governments never like to be meddled with. But it happens to be the whole idea of the American political system.

Having won in the Supreme Court, the press now must fight the more insidious self-censorship that comes when it tries to avoid future confrontations, when it concedes in the newsroom what it won in the courts. Better than Roger L'Estrange is the more contemporary wisdom of Elmer Davis, who said in the height of the Joe McCarthy era:

Don't let them scare you. For the men who are trying to do that to us are scared themselves. They are afraid that what they think will not stand critical examination; they are afraid that the principles on which this Republic was founded and has been conducted are wrong. They will tell you that there is a hazard in the freedom of the mind and of course there is, as in any freedom. In trying to think right you run the risk of thinking wrong. But there is no hazard at all, no uncertainty, in letting somebody else tell you what to think; that is sheer damnation.

3   PR Infiltrates the Press

A friend of mine runs a clipping service whose staff looks every day at every page of every daily newspaper published in the United States. He therefore has a remarkably broad if somewhat glassy-eyed view of what is printed in the American press. Some time ago I asked him what percentage of nonadvertising matter ("news") in dailies is public relations material or purely the output of the news source itself. He pointed to a pile of papers and said: "Pick one out."

From the middle of the deck, at random, I pulled out a paper of more than fifty thousand circulation that would justifiably be on any reasonable list of the country's fifty best. My friend dissected it while I watched. Comparing what he knew to be public relations releases with stories whose internal evidence made it obvious that the news-generating outlet itself was the sole source of information, he found that 82 percent of the paper's nonadvertising matter—local, wire and syndicate—originated completely, or virtually completely, with the news source itself.

That some news is the voice of the source alone, untouched, is not surprising or bad. That so little of a good newspaper's content shows independent initiative and development seemed strange for an industry that hires fifty thousand full-time editors and reporters. This did not surprise my friend but it did me.

But even this experience was insufficient preparation for the 1963

hearings of Senator J. William Fulbright and his Senate Foreign Relations Committee into what was formally called "Activities of Non-
diplomatic Representatives of Foreign Principals in the United
States"; that is, public relations and lobbying in this country for
foreign clients. The investigation looked into a few public relations
concerns representing foreign governments and companies—the
Hamilton Wright Organization, Selvage & Lee, Julius Klein—and,
inevitably, into their relations with American news.

News organizations themselves seemed to enjoy privileged sanc-
tuary at the hearings. Whether for fear of offending, or because it
seemed contrary to the First Amendment or secondary to his purpose, the Senator did not engage in hot pursuit of the press. But
enough emerged to give American news organizations pause. Not
many, however, paused long enough to report fully the proceedings'
evidence of commercialism in the news selection process.

Pursuing some of the evidence brings to light a kind of PR-in-the-
press that a large number of editors consider harmless and profitable
fun. One day in November 1952, for example, the *Miami Herald*
ran a story without credit and therefore seemingly its own: "Somehow
dahlias, daisies, pine trees and 65-degree weather aren't the picture
most people visualize when they think of a tropical country like the
Dominican Republic. Yet this is just what . . ."

Two weeks later the *Hartford Courant* ran, also seemingly on its
own:

"Somehow dahlias, daisies, pine trees and 65-degree weather
aren't the picture . . ."

This, of course, was tourism puffery (which, even so, bears significant political benefits for the country involved) taken unaltered
from a foreign-government handout. For some reason editors regard
this, along with women's page, financial page and entertainment page
puffery, as ethically sound and no disservice to the reader.

A couple of years after the dahlias and daisies appeared to sprout
indigenously (in many more papers than just those of Miami and
Hartford) there appeared an editorial, seemingly locally written, in
the late *Montpelier Evening Argus*: "Donna Maria Martinez Trujillo,
wife of Generalissimo Rafael L. Trujillo, the fabulous four-time
president of the Dominican Republic, has written a book . . ."

This laudatory editorial, word for word, was printed also in Zanesville, Ohio, and in other papers from Calais, Maine, to Deming, New Mexico. All appeared to be local editors' opinions of an obscure book.

A year after that the *New Bedford Standard-Times* ran an editorial, seeming to be locally written: "Today the Dominican Republic . . . is a bulwark of strength against Communism and has been widely cited as one of the cleanest, healthiest, happiest countries on the globe. Guiding spirit of this fabulous transformation is Generalissimo Trujillo who worked tirelessly . . ."

At about the same time a small weekly in Mooresville, North Carolina, ran an editorial called "What a Great and Good Ruler Can Accomplish for a Country," and it began with what seemed the Mooresville editor's analysis: "Today the Dominican Republic . . . is a bulwark of strength against Communism and has been widely cited as one of the cleanest, healthiest, happiest . . ."

The innocuous dahlias and daisies were gifts from Trujillo's New York agent, the late Harry Klemfuss. The editorial on the book of Mrs. Trujillo, wife of the fabulous four-time president, was also compliments of Mr. Klemfuss through the services of a syndicate called U.S. Press Association, Inc., which received $125 from Klemfuss to send out the editorial to its list of 1,300 dailies and weeklies (who get a batch of editorials free every week). The "cleanest, healthiest, happiest" country editorial came via the same route with the help of $125 of Trujillo's money. The Montpelier paper had two other editorials on the page with the one urging purchase of Mrs. Trujillo's book. One editorial advised readers to use reflectorized tape on their car bumpers to prevent accidents; the other told how American baby foods had produced good in the world. These last two were also with the compliments of U.S. Press Association (which had been paid $125 each by manufacturers, respectively, of reflectorized tape and of American baby foods). For those interested, U.S. Press Association later raised its fee to $175 to get editorials into local papers and the proprietor, Robert Nelson Taylor, says he sends out only conservative editorials and does not serve papers he considers liberal or Democratic.

If one looked further into the activities of Trujillo's publicity agent, one finds that on September 13, 1955, the *New Orleans Item* carried an interview in New Orleans with Klemfuss in which the paid agent of Trujillo praised the leader as an outstanding fighter against communism in the Western hemisphere. The story was written, but not signed, by a reporter for the *Item*, Roland Von Kurnatowski, who, according to Klemfuss records and his own admission, was paid more than $500 by Klemfuss to place this and other pro-Trujillo stories in the *Item*. Kurnatowski was the *Item*'s Latin American editor. He says the paper knew and approved of his relations with Klemfuss and Trujillo.

If, further, one inspected the Klemfuss file in the Foreign Agents Registration Section of the Department of Justice one would find that in 1958 there were two provocative entries about Trujillo expenditures in the United States: "August, 1958 . . . United Press reporting assignment, $75," and "June 20, INS Special Services Division, $226.20." And thereby hangs a tale.

Senator Fulbright drew out part of this tale. Hearst's International News Service, before its purchase by United Press, turned over its reporters to commercial clients who paid a fee. The reporters would ask news sources questions the private client ordered and put together a report. For additional fees, INS put the client's material on its news wire—or at least the records of the Trujillo regime indicate that INS did this for him at $2,000 a month and offered to continue to send Trujillo material as news to its wire service customers under the by-line of an INS editor.

This arrangement paralleled another Trujillo news alliance in this country. On February 5, 1959, an agent of Trujillo handed $750,000 in cash to Alexander L. Guterma, president of the Mutual Broadcasting System, in return for which Guterma agreed to have Mutual broadcast to the American people every day a minimum of 14 minutes of "news" desired by Trujillo. Guterma ultimately went to jail and Mutual stopped the agreement. INS never made so large a haul, so far as the record shows, but it did offer for sale both its reporters and space on its "news" tickers.

United Press became United Press International when it absorbed INS in 1958, but for at least a generation it, too, had had a Special Service Bureau, which also made its reporters and photographers available to nonjournalistic clients. It has now stopped this. There is no evidence that UPI ever put the client reports on its news wires.

But the committee put in the record such UPI promotional letters as this:

Do you know that United Press International, through its Special Service Bureau, can obtain authoritative and completely accurate information to help solve your decision-making problems? Through this Bureau the reporting facilities of the world's largest news gathering organizations are made available to private industry on a commercial basis. UPI reporters on the scene can interview the proper official . . .

The editor of UPI later said that the wire service would let reporter and subject know when inquiry was made for a private client, that it would undertake no tasks for foreign governments and that client material never had been put on the UPI wire and never would be.

One major public relations operator in Washington told me why he used UPI's Special Service Bureau for taking PR photographs—of clients signing government contracts or conferring with cabinet members.

There are a hundred of these affairs going on in Washington every day and it's a lucky man who can get an editor to look at one. If I hired a commercial photographer it would be the next day before he could deliver the glossy and at UPI I'd have to stand in line at the picture editor's desk. When I used UPI to take the PR shot their own photographer processed the shot the same day, along with his news pictures, and he dropped my shot on the picture editor's desk. I really don't think the picture editor picked our PR shot because his own photographer took it. But what made the difference was that we were in the UPI shop the same day as the event and we knew our picture would be on the picture editor's desk among the candidates. That's the biggest single hurdle and using UPI Special Service took care of it. About a year ago UPI told us the PR work was interfering with their getting news shots and they transferred the whole PR operation to an outside commercial outfit. This took away the advantage of using UPI and I haven't used it since.

There is an important technical meaning to UPI's Special Service Bureau assignments in Washington because, in a sense, the existence of the Bureau could impede UPI's freedom of journalistic movement in the capital on its conventional rounds. The basic accreditation in Washington is to the Congressional Press Gallery, Rule 2 of which states: "Members of the Press Galleries of Congress shall not, as long as they remain members of the Gallery, engage in paid advertising, publicity, or promotion work for any individual, corporation or organization."

This rule is taken seriously by the Gallery's Standing Committee, which is composed of correspondents operating by sufferance of Congress. Six years ago Standing Committee questions led to the resignation, temporarily, of Marguerite Higgins, then of the *New York Herald Tribune,* while she promoted a toothpaste. Somewhat later Drew Pearson had to promise to stop plugging a throat gargle. As a result of the Fulbright hearings, the Standing Committee reprimanded Glen Everett, correspondent for Religious News Service, because he had prepared a memo for Selvage & Lee, a PR firm.

One of the troublesome aspects of UPI's Special Service Bureau is that some UPI correspondents in Washington did not even know it existed until they read about the Fulbright hearings. Neither did the senators, some of whom plainly had misgivings. By their questions they showed concern over past relations with UPI correspondents to whom they might conceivably have given confidential information while the correspondent, unknowingly, was really on a private mission for a political enemy. UPI says this has not happened. But in state capitals, UPI Special Services has contracted to ask key state legislators their intentions on banking legislation, on behalf of a nonjournalistic client with interests in banking laws.

The possibilities are disturbing, especially in the light of an exchange between Fulbright and C. Edmonds Allen, manager of UPI's Special Service Bureau. They were talking about UPI doing chores for public relations firms.

FULBRIGHT: You take no responsibility as to who their clients are?
ALLEN: That is correct, sir.
FULBRIGHT: And therefore, certainly your reporters could not know who they are working for in performing an assignment given to them by Special Services, could they?
ALLEN: That is correct, sir.
FULBRIGHT: And also, therefore, the person whom the person [reporter] is contacting in the course of his assignment naturally wouldn't know either, would he?
ALLEN: That is correct.

No one brought up at the hearing a major danger in selling reporters' entrées: the power to make things happen merely by asking questions. UPI charges its private clients fifty dollars a month retainer and a per-assignment fee. It could be worth several times fifty dollars for private parties—corporations, business associations, labor unions —to have a national wire service ask a pointed question of a key government official. The act of a national news organization in asking a question has one primary meaning to an experienced news source: This matter is in danger of becoming hot national news. No matter what the answer, or if there is no answer at all, the political status quo after the question is not the same as it was before.

There is a recognized danger in any news gatherer's being under obligation to a news source. When UPI's editor said he would fire a reporter who did public relations work on the side, Senator Fulbright looked up in blue-eyed innocence and said gently:

"I don't understand why . . . you don't feel that way about UPI itself."

Public relations firms play a substantial role in the world of news, as both they and news organizations are forever reiterating. It is perfectly obvious that the job of collecting the day's news must include public relations offerings. But this is legitimate, so far as significant news and obligation to the reader is concerned, only if the press is knowing, discriminating and ruthless in its selection of such material.

What happens when the news gatherer is under contract to serve Stan the PR man when he has cash in hand at the same time that he is under moral obligation to be ruthless with Stan the PR man when he appears with press release in hand—or more realistically, when Stan the PR man's client is involved, along with many less articulate parties in a news situation?

The traditional defense of a double standard has been that when the news gatherer puts on his news hat he then proceeds to bite the hand that feeds him. UPI does not let its reporters individually test this thesis but apparently sees no ethical problem in committing the reporters as a body. One is reminded that when some old pals from the past showed up at the White House to rake in a bit of patronage, a newly installed President walked in and announced:

"Gentlemen, Chet Arthur of New York and Chester A. Arthur,

President of the United States, are two different persons. Good day."

UPI was further embarrassed when names of a couple of its editors appeared as beneficiaries of the sources whose material they put out as UPI service. Jack Woliston, feature editor of UPI News Service, was the subject of letters by a major PR operator, Hamilton Wright, to Mexican and South African government clients urging them to give Woliston free vacations. "On a recent visit to Mexico," Wright told South Africa, "one of these editors wrote five stories—used another five written by us and literally flooded the U.S.A. with excellent photographs about tourism in Mexico. This man is Jack Woliston, Executive News Editor, United Press International of New York. . . . We have approached Mr. Woliston about a trip to South Africa. The answer is 'yes.' It is 'yes,' to his superiors."

On January 27, 1961, Wright urged the government of Mexico to give another UPI editor a free trip to that country. "He is: Harold Blumenfeld, Editor of UPI News Photos . . . and Mrs. Blumenfeld . . . They are using our pictures on Mexico regularly." Wright's office records show that Wright paid $1,500 for the Blumenfelds' vacation. Neither man refuted his testimony, though given an opportunity.

If UPI was embarrassed by such exposure it may be because the printed media—the old INS excepted—set themselves higher standards than, for example, the theater newsreels, which also figured in the testimony.

By any standards of ethics and news selection, the United States must have the most slovenly newsreels in the world. It is almost impossible to see a newsreel in an American movie house that does not have a commercial plug carried as news. Some are entirely press agentry. And it pays.

Hamilton Wright, an expert in supplying grist for this mill, says a "documentary" or short subject may cost his foreign client $10,000 to $50,000 to produce. He then sells this to a major film distributor for one dollar. The film distributor in turn sells it for profit to movie houses for varying rentals. Or the PR firm, or a foreign government directly, may pay a distributing outfit a flat fee, on the order of $2.50 to $12.50 per placement, to get the PR film run on local television stations. The odds are overwhelming that any slack time—and perhaps a prime time—"documentary" seen on local television was made and paid for by someone looking for free publicity or public indoctrination. In most cases there is no indication who made the film. The relationship between the men who decide what will be seen by the public and the PR firms who want them to peddle the stuff is extraordinarily congenial. Jack Kuhne selects short-subject films for Twentieth Century-Fox and is a friend of Hamilton Wright's. When Wright made some foreign propaganda films, two of Kuhne's sons were used on the crew, one at $250 a week, the other at $600. Max Klein, of MGM News of the Day and Hearst Metrotone News, was put forward by Wright for a free trip to Mexico with his wife because, Wright informed Mexico, "He has used every single newsreel story we have sent him on Mexico." Klein, in acknowledging the free vacation plans, told Wright: "I intend to keep this sub rosa."

The status of Nationalist China and the offshore islands is a delicate one and on occasion has threatened the peace. Charles Baily, short-subject sales manager for Warner Brothers, planning what to tell the film audience about the issue, wrote to Wright, who was getting about $300,000 a year from the Nationalist Chinese government to push its line: "You know what we can use and I will leave it to your judgment."

This congeniality between ax-grinders and "news" executives extended to feature syndicates. Louis Messolonghetis, of King Features Syndicate, was entertained by Mexico. To assure Mexico that the vacation had paid off, Wright sent them tearsheets of an eight-column newspaper feature page on Mexico sent out by King Features. Courtland Smith, an editor of Central Press Association, a branch of King Features, himself sent proofs to Mexico "to show how we have made good use of Hamilton Wright's photos on half a dozen occasions during recent weeks. These particular pages were included in our service to nearly 100 daily papers throughout the United States. The feature story went to more than 200."

The next day Smith wrote to Wright: "Dear Ham, We had a terrific week in Mexico . . . The suite at the Hilton was lavish . . . You told me the government would pick up the full tab, so we signed for everything." On another occasion Smith told Wright that to accommodate a request by the Nationalist China PR man, Smith would eliminate the signs that the material originated as PR for a foreign government and would substitute "the large KFS slug you said might be helpful."

These executives are gatekeepers of American news. PR men who know the field know that they are far more important than the editors of individual newspapers, not only because they can dump their material into news channels wholesale, which they do, but also because the material usually reaches the individual newspaper, magazine or station with the slug of the distributing organization—implying that it is the result of their own initiative and reporting. As Hamilton Wright told his client, Nationalist China:

This material will be released direct to the following syndicates who service 95 per cent of all the newspapers in the U.S.A. These syndicates "sell" their services to the largest and smallest newspapers, supplying them with pictures (wirephotos), Sunday features, articles on every subject, rotogravure layouts, etc. We have worked with these editors for more than 35 years. They know us—we know them. In 75 per cent of the releases, neither the editor of the newspaper—nor the newspaper reader— HAS ANY KNOWLEDGE WHERE THE MATERIAL ORIGINATED. Only the editor of the syndicate knows.

The uppercase letters are Mr. Wright's.

Mr. Wright is prone to exaggerate. For example, he claimed that every foot of newsreel film from Nationalist China and the offshore islands seen anywhere in the United States, in movie houses or on television, for a period of five crucial years was straight PR processed by him. He is not strictly accurate on this. Not *every* bit was his, only most of it.

PR-in-the-news cannot be dismissed as merely a self-serving fantasy created by public relations men intent on promoting themselves with unearned credit. There is much of this, to be sure, and PR clients are notoriously gullible to the meaningless scrapbook and inflated claims of influence. But the impact of press agentry in the news is all too real. There is too much evidence of effective tainting of the wellsprings and conduits of news. The largely anonymous men who control the syndicate and wire service copy desks and the central wirephoto machines determine at a single decision what millions will see and hear. Whether they are properly trained and selected for this responsibility—and many of them are less discriminating than editors on individual papers who must work with what these gatekeepers send them—is one issue. But there seems little doubt that these gate-keepers preside over an operation in which an appalling amount of press agentry sneaks in the back door of American journalism and marches untouched out the front door as "news."

Some clandestine PR operations put local editors at a severe disadvantage. The Fulbright committee determined that the PR firm of Selvage & Lee, under a contract with Portuguese interests to spend up to $500,000 a year on pushing the line that Portuguese administration of the African colonies of Angola and Mozambique was enlightened and happy, created a dummy "Portuguese-American" committee in Boston and then used it as a lobbying and pressure group. When Senator Gore of Tennessee made a speech asking that American guns not be used in killing Africans, the Washington office of Selvage & Lee composed a letter to the editor implying that the Senator was arguing against anticommunism in Africa and stating explicitly that this was the letter of an American citizen group. It sent the letter to Boston to have it mailed to 162 newspapers in districts where Senator Gore ran for election. It also ran a letter campaign against Philip Potter of the *Baltimore Sun*. Against this type of operation editors can exercise only normal skepticism and rules of relevancy.

But it is not all so blind or unwitting. The National Editorial Association, NEA (not to be confused with the syndicate Newspaper Enterprise Association, no relation), represents 6,200 smaller papers in the country, including five hundred dailies. In January 1963 they sent a junket of more than fifty newspaper editors through Africa, where Selvage & Lee paid for the trip through Angola. Attached to the trip and identified as representing the *"South Sioux City* (Nebraska) *Star"* was Paul Wagner, who was of great help to his fellow newspapermen in deciding what to see and what it meant. He provided them with fact sheets and stories about conditions in Angola. Wagner had been the publisher of the small Nebraska paper until 1951. But he was now an account executive for Selvage & Lee and a paid propagandist for the Portuguese interests in Angola.

After that, Selvage & Lee purchased at something under $2,500 a two-page spread in NEA's publication, *Publishers' Auxiliary*, to run rhapsodic pieces in news type by NEA editors and by Wagner himself, all of them on the wonders of life and the times in Angola (but nothing from the few editors on the junket who caught on to the PR operation and objected).

This is not a freak combination of what purports to be a serious editorial association of newspapers and direct PR insertion into the news. *Publishers' Auxiliary* regularly runs a service for PR firms, corporations, utility industries and others, whereby a mat—a pressed cardboard mold into which hot type metal is poured to reproduce pictures and texts cheaply—will be sent to anyone on the fourteen thousand papers receiving the publication who asks for it, this mat being a PR plug for the product or publicity line of the firm that pays *Publishers' Auxiliary*. This is nothing clandestine. It is free to the newspaper; it plugs something any editor of normal intelligence can detect; and two previous handlers get paid to send it out. As an executive for Selvage & Lee said of the editors who get such material and print it:

"The people who print it . . . they know that they are getting it free. . . . They are not so naïve."

It may be time for the executives of great news organizations to reconsider the role of public relations in the news. Public relations is useful but it has taken over some editorial functions. That it would try to do this is inevitable and it must be said that public relations men are far clearer in their objectives than are editors and publishers. The PR men are bound to further the interests of their clients and they, at least, are doing what they are getting paid to do. They don't have the responsibility of editors and news executives, who arrogate to themselves a crucial and exalted position in American democracy and who insist they exist and are paid primarily to protect the readers' interests in a fair presentation of the significant news.

PR is not going to disappear. But one first step in keeping it under control might be an intense course for newspapermen and editors on the way PR actually works. This would include not just the sociological treatises on publicity but some of the back-door minuets glimpsed briefly in the Fulbright hearings.

The news editor today is lighting manager of a stage from which the audience hears innumerable wild sounds and the thump of falling bodies. To illuminate this multifarious action intelligibly is difficult at best. It is so difficult that the lighting manager is often bedeviled by a peculiar habit on the news stage: some of the actors carry their own spotlights. These actors, like good PR men, turn their lights on themselves when they look good, often at considerable expense to themselves and with many asides to the audience on how much light they contribute to this shadowy world. There are times, however, when the actors are up to some villainy or else their suspenders have just broken, at which point they prudently turn off their light or shine it at someone else. Thus, at the most crucial points in the news drama, PR men are paid to prevent exposure of the client when he is in trouble; the press is paid to do precisely the opposite. This is so obvious that some of the press have forgotten it.

There were many ironies in the Fulbright hearings. One was that despite some of the dubious techniques of the PR men, they came out looking better than the press, because technically they obviously were doing an effective job to attain their ends and too many in the press were doing a deficient job in pursuing theirs.

Further, publications and broadcasters are plainly giving away something they should sell—advertising. Hamilton Wright promised China six dollars of free news space in American media for every dollar China paid him. (He also told China to keep this quiet, maybe because he offered South Africa only five to one.)

Beyond that, the failures of the system were brought out by a congressional committee, gentle though it was to the press, and not by the press itself. If any reforms come from it, they follow outside exposure, not self-policing. This does not bode well for the traditional insistence that government should leave the press alone because the press can govern itself.

The final irony was that not so long ago many news organizations were complaining bitterly, and sometimes justifiably, that their own government was managing the news. And yet large news organizations, central in our system of information, not only did not seem to mind but actively assisted (and profited financially) when news to the American people was managed by foreign governments and private special pleaders.

4   The Gentle Suppression

\#

A dramatist looking for a tableau entitled "Dynamic Democracy in Action" might have chosen the sidewalk in front of the White House a few years ago during a civil rights disturbance. At the east end of the block were hundreds of civil rights picketers with signs urging protection of blacks in Alabama. At the west end was a lone uniformed storm trooper of the American Nazi party carrying a placard with the legend, "Who Needs Niggers?", protected by two large serene black policemen.

The Nazis, led by the late George Lincoln Rockwell, were a standard irritant in Washington. Rockwell was a shrewd manipulator of events to dramatize his cause. For years his troopers picketed the White House with shocking signs, peddling Hitlerian propaganda, haranguing tourists with boasts to build bigger and better gas chambers to kill Jews, and breaking up public meetings. Nazis ran onto the stage of the National Theater. They broke into convention meetings in downtown hotels. They disrupted a large gathering at American University by grabbing the stage microphone to yell, "Sieg Heil," and pushed the speaker off the platform while Nazis spotted throughout the audience began fist fights. They interfered with sessions of the United States Congress, sometimes unfurling banners and shouting Nazi slogans from the gallery of the House and Senate, once grabbing the microphone during a congressional hearing, and another time running onto the floor of the House of Representatives dressed in blackface.

Individual Nazis have had less public dealings with the police. One group handcuffed young Jewish boys to headquarters furniture. Others, to the dismay of their führer, seemed unable to understand the statutory rape law.

All in all, the Nazis qualified as news—at the most as a gang promoting savagery and paranoia on the national scene, and at the least as civic pests. But the three Washington papers, in varying degrees, applied a special test for hard news about Nazi activities. Theirs was not an absolute quarantine; all three papers ran numerous accounts of Nazi episodes and printed background pieces. Yet the Nazis got special handling, with the conscious objective of denying them publicity and minimizing their impact. Sometimes this meant not printing news of an event; New York papers and the wire services carried Washington items about the Nazis that were not carried in the local papers. Or it meant omitting parts of the news considered useful to the Nazis in spreading their message. Both the *New York Times* and the *Washington Post,* for example, carried stories in October 1960 of Nazi picketing at the Democratic National Committee headquarters in the capital, but the *Post* omitted what the Nazi placards read while the *Times* printed them ("Kikes for Kennedy"). When a Nazi jumped on the stage of the National Theater, the *Washington Daily News* did not report it and the *Post* did, but buried it in the last two paragraphs of a story on the normal proceedings in the theater. There is little doubt that Washington editors try to run news of the Nazis as little as possible and, when they do, to minimize any advantage to the Nazis and produce the most "healthy" reaction among readers.

These Washington editors are among the most sophisticated in the business, and they have one of the most discerning newspaper audiences in the country. They give individual attention to each story about the Nazis as it occurs. It is a quarantine under the best possible conditions of a subject odious to most Americans. But the quarantine is still pernicious.

News quarantines—exclusion of subjects from news columns because they may produce harmful effects—are difficult to discuss clearly. They fall under the editorial discretion that must be the right of every editor. They are considered a sign of one of the enlightened

developments in American journalism, the idea of social responsibility in the press. At the same time, they are often indistinguishable
from less attractive practices, such as special treatment of sacred
cows or suppressions for the benefit of friends of the paper. But even
when quarantines are altruistically imposed, they interfere with the
democratic process and are demoralizing to the discipline of news
judgment.

Prevention of racial tension is the most common contemporary
cause of local quarantines. They have been practiced in both North
and South when black-white incidents occur. Chicago for a time had
a ban on reporting racial disturbances. In Washington, D.C., a spectacular riot in the municipal stadium was at first unreported, then
distorted to make it appear nonracial. There is no question that at
the moment these embargoes seemed prudent.

But not so long ago most Southern dailies had a quarantine in
their general news columns on any items that made blacks look good
or normal. In these papers blacks did not get born, win scholarships,
get elected to lodge offices or die in respectability; they only committed abhorrent crimes and led depraved lives. All the editors of
such papers I ever talked to insisted that they were only reporting
news the community needed to know.

When civil rights became an issue, many segregationist editors censored out news of integrationist agitation, believing they were doing it
for the good of the community. Other editors censored out news of
segregationist agitation, believing they were doing it for the good of
the community. Both kinds of editors sometimes did it at the same
time in the same towns, as in Nashville and Little Rock during their
troubles. These papers had decided what was good for the community
and then trimmed their news to fit that end, though the ends were
opposite.

Needless to say, race relations has not been the only subject of
quarantines. For many years papers in heavily Catholic areas printed
almost nothing about birth control. Trouble in religious groups, even
spectacular public trouble, has come under fierce pressure for suppression. In Boston a fiery Jesuit, Father Feeney, defied his arch-
bishop, spoke against diocesan activity, was excommunicated, and
formed his own schismatic order, which held anti-Semitic rallies on
Boston Common, sometimes with violence. But readers of the Boston

papers remained ignorant of almost the entire Feeney story. The church wanted no news of its embarrassment and Jews wanted no spreading of anti-Semitic appeals, both urging a quarantine for the public good.

Nor is this practice limited to the United States. (It goes without saying that in countries with a controlled press the quarantine is found in its pristine form.) Once, the management of the Quebec papers *Le Soleil* and *L'Événement,* according to *Editor & Publisher,* "banned publication of statements preaching violence by separatists, nationalists and other groups considered to have no authority or groups considered not representative of the public interest." It is language one expects in a code issued by Louis XIV, but there is no reason to doubt that the general manager of the papers felt he was acting for the public good, or as he put it, "to serve the best interests of the milieu with which they are identified."

To argue against quarantines one has to admit risk. Printing news of bad events often makes the events worse. Giving news space to a demagogue grants him his heart's desire. Reporting "events" deliberately created in order to exploit the news process rewards the schemers and imagemakers.

But how can the editor ignore all planned events? If he did there would be almost no political news, because if there is one thing a politician plots day and night it is how to exploit the news process, and this goes from the President down to the Rockwells. News events that are not acts of God are acts of men, and of men who have planned shrewdly. Inspired events need not be reported indiscriminately, but they cannot be dismissed indiscriminately.

Should the reporter and editor be responsible for the ill effects of printing truthful news? If so, then each editor and reporter has to decide ahead of time what he wants the reader to think and do, and report only those events that lead the reader to that end. Yet what is one editor's bad effect may be another's glory: in Nashville and Little Rock two leading editors wanted differing kinds of society, and so reported different kinds of news.

The pursuers of domestic justice are safer putting their trust in an open society and professional discipline rather than in the wisdom and powers of prophecy of any individual—even a reporter or editor.

In the end, the journalist's responsibility is to the reader, not to history, and the heart of that responsibility is to give the reader as clear a picture of pertinent reality as he can, based on how the reporter sees it at that particular moment. Reality is a big word and a subjective one at that. But for journalists it boils down to the reporter's seeing the world with his own eyes and not someone else's. When he begins to filter what he sees and reports through a concern whether the reader will react "correctly," he has ceased being a reporter. The exception, of course, is the existence of a clear and present danger to life and order in the community, but genuinely clear and present dangers arising from the printing of news are rare in any editor's lifetime.

Promoters of quarantines, when they are not the editors themselves, are usually responsible men doing good works. A few years ago a Jewish group circularized editors, asking for a blackout of news about bigots:

"Bigots are not deterred by expressions of public disapproval but often thrive on them; publishing scurrilous statements by bigots, even to ridicule them, only gives such statements respectability; publicizing the bigot, even unfavorably, inflates him."

About George Lincoln Rockwell and the Nazis, the memorandum said:

"It is as an advocate of nazism that Rockwell demands a hearing. But is nazism an issue in this country? Should anyone urging a Hitler regime for the United States be taken seriously as the exponent of one 'side' of a valid public question?"

The concern here is too much with the gratification of the bigot at seeing his name in the newspapers. Men on the way to their executions have been pleased to see their picture in the paper but their joy has not saved them. And if news space shall be given only to ideas considered respectable, then authority (which grants respectability) censors the press.

Nor is it true that Rockwell and others like him deserve news space only as advocates. They deserve it, when they deserve it at all, as principals in public events affecting others. The fact that they deliberately provoke such events does not necessarily mean that the events are not news. If a mayor douses his hair with lighter fluid and makes a flaming leap from a persimmon tree singing "Dixie," it may be a stunt but it is news. If a Nazi deliberately breaks up a public meeting by pushing the speaker off the stage, it is a device to get publicity but it is news. (Papers that are worried about the impact of the Nazis might have played the news straight and then asked editorially why the Nazis arrested for breaking up the meeting were let off with a ten-dollar forfeiture of collateral and never brought to trial.)

Who is to decide whether Nazism is an issue in this country? And how is anyone to know, if it is quarantined from public study? If it is not an issue, then there is no danger in playing news of Nazis in the normal way. The fact that there is a quarantine means editors accept that Nazism is an issue with enough people to cause worry. Rockwell was not an ordinary soapbox shouter. At one time he had the backing of a man with $4 million. He was able to disrupt sessions of Congress. He had only a couple dozen loutish troopers but he was a resourceful leader who had been the subject of many man-hours of official worry by the Department of Justice, the metropolitan police and the district commissioners, and of unofficial attention by university officials and by American Civil Liberties Union leaders preparing defenses of the Nazis' constitutional rights while worrying how to accomplish this without infringing the rights of others. These are deliberations of a fundamental kind from which principles and practices evolve that are applied to all society. If the elite were worried about Rockwell as a problem, the citizen ought to have worried, too. If the elite think the citizenry may come out the wrong way, then what is needed is more news, not less.

In 1960 a wave of desecrations of Jewish temples took place in Germany and the United States. In city after city there was an epidemic of swastikas splashed onto walls and windows—about 650 were reported to police. After it was all over, two social scientists, David Caplovitz and Candace Rogers, wrote an analysis for the Anti-Defamation League with this conclusion on the effects of news reports:

It cannot be disputed that publicity given to the German desecrations and subsequent outbreaks here played a major role in setting off further incidents. The offenders themselves, as we saw earlier, often reported that they got the idea from the newspapers, from television, and other mass media. It is probable that as early incidents mounted, publicity given to them precipitated other incidents as offenders of otherwise low predisposition were stimulated to participate. But it would be unwise to conclude from this fact alone that the media should refrain from publishing information of such events.

In the first place, the outbreak received more than one kind of publicity. In addition to informing the public that the incidents had occurred, the media also published reactions to the outbreak—and the reactions were uniformly negative. Religious, civic and political leaders alike condemned the incidents in the strongest terms. Regardless of the actual level of anti-Semitism the epidemic represented, it called forth a unanimous denunciation of religious intolerance and a public reaffirmation of the principles of brotherhood. We do not know what long-range effects the reiteration of this public morality may have. It is possible that once the crisis has passed, the feelings and expressions of solidarity it evoked passed also, without touching more subtle and pervasive expressions of prejudice in housing, employment, and recreation. But it is also possible that because of the crisis itself, new agencies of cooperation were created, dormant patterns of collaboration reactivated, and the Jewish community was reassured about the goodwill of its neighbors. . . .

In some unknown proportion of cases, the swastika outbreak may well have given specific form and content to vague and diffuse hostilities, so that offenders who were not orginally anti-Semitic have, in the course of the outbreak, learned about the prevalence—and for some, the legitimacy —of religious and ethnic intolerance. Their hostilities now have a new specific target. Others, however, who began with relatively mild and vague anti-Semitic sentiments, may well have been startled and abashed by the violent reaction their offenses provoked, learning that in this area at least, what seemed to them a legitimate and mild form of hostility is in fact a major transgression in the eyes of society. Just as the epidemic may have taught some to be anti-Semitic, it may have taught others not to be.

5   Alas, The Small-Town Press

\#

The unperishing myth of American journalism is the ideal of the small-town newspaper as the grass-roots opinionmaker of the nation, the last bastion of personal journalism, the final arena where a single human being can mold a community with his fearless iconoclasm.

Needless to say, there are some small papers like this and they are marvels to behold. But the fact is that most small dailies and weeklies are the backyard of the trade, repositories for any piece of journalistic junk tossed over the fence, run as often by printshop proprietors as by editors. Mostly they serve as useful bulletin boards of births, deaths and marriages (providing this news comes in by its own initiative); only in exceptional cases do they raise and resolve important local issues. When it comes to transmitting signals from the outside world, a remarkable number of these papers convey pure—that is, unadulterated—press agentry. Its subject matter, which is printed both as "news" and as editorial comment, ranges from mouthwash to politics—usually right wing.

Few readers realize that the publicity pipelines supplying the small papers are numerous, gushing and free. A dozen large syndicates provide such material without charge to local papers, sometimes in printed or mimeographed form but more often in mats. These syndicates make their money by charging a fee to the propagandists who have something to sell. Some businesses and other organizations bypass the syndicates and send out their own canned goods to be reproduced as local products.

For years the National Association of Manufacturers has sent out editorials, which have been picked up, usually verbatim, by six hundred daily newspapers, most often without attribution to the NAM as source. The AFL-CIO sends out its material, too, but with far less success. In 1962 Medicare was the subject of a syndicated and boiler plate battle, with a volunteer pro-Medicare group sending out through a commercial syndicate (at a cost of about $15,000) canned material, some of it from officials of the Department of Health, Education and Welfare. In response, the American Medical Association used the usual syndicate channels, plus three articles that it sent to local medical affiliates, which presented them personally to their local papers. Anti-Medicare editorials appeared with miraculous similarity in widely separated places. In a two-month period, for example, newspapers in South Carolina, Montana and Michigan all ran editorials beginning: "Remember the Medicare proposal of the Kennedy Administration? It got nowhere. . . ."

But there is nothing like a political balance in the battle of boiler plate, the standard, prefabricated pictures-and-text distributed to the media. In 1962 the *American Press,* a trade magazine for small dailies and weeklies, polled a cross section of such papers and found that 84 percent opposed any government-sponsored medical or hospital aid to the aged, were strongly opposed to federal aid to education and were generally found in the right-wing Republican camp. The vast body of opinion picked up word for word by small papers is either strictly commercial or ultraconservative.

The reader, of course, is almost never told that he is seeing something other than the considered product of his local editor.

There persists the image of the hard-fighting small-town editor, working late at night, his green eyeshade low, his fingers spasmodically attacking the typewriter, his mind anticipating the angry reaction to his words by people he will have to face in the street, but deciding it is his moral duty to speak his mind. But behold what happens more often. The man is at his desk, all right, but if it is a very small paper, the editor is also the owner, ad salesman and mailer. And he is not processing issues and words through his mind. He has before him a dummy of page two—the girdle ad on the right, the tractor ad on the left, the annual American Legion carnival stepped between them, and nine inches of remaining space reserved for "news." It is not his mind that is creating and discriminating for this space. It is more likely his right hand, fishing through the purple mats and yellow mimeographed canned editorials in his lower drawer, feeling for one exactly nine column-inches long. Depending on the fortuitous length and the luck of his fingers, what will triumph on page two the next day may be an article proclaiming the virtues of prune juice for regularity (compliments of the prune industry) or an editorial condemning labor unions (compliments of a conservative lobby). This is not to say that the local editor disagrees with the prune juice or the social doctrine; one must assume that he does not. But the errand boy of the precast words of a public relations man who happened to plug his product in exactly nine inches somehow seems disappointing as the hero figure of American journalism.

One of the commercial conduits for the canned editorial, but not the largest, is the U.S. Press Association, Inc., which has a cosmic sound enhanced by the parenthetical note next to its address: ("12 mi. from the WHITE HOUSE"). It is a friendly family business, once run by a pleasant couple in McLean, Virginia. Mr. and Mrs. Robert Nelson Taylor and their successors would take your words and ideas, if they approved of them, and $175 of your money, and send your editorial message, free of charge, to 1,199 weeklies and 150 dailies. The Taylors didn't hide from the local editor that he was getting conservative editorials that someone else had paid for. According to a standing box on top of the weekly batch of editorials:

This regular, comprehensive service is made possible by responsible American Business Institutions who pay an established fee to present timely business stories of FREE ENTERPRISE to Grass-Roots Americans, "The Most Influential People in the World." Clients do not dictate policy. . . . OUR OPINIONS REMAIN OUR OWN. [The Taylors' devotion to old-fashioned Capitalism includes unashamed deployment of Capital Letters.]

In a brochure inviting clients to buy its service, U.S. Press offers them a measure of freedom of opinion: "EASY TO USE . . . Just give us your story, in conference or by mail or phone. WE DO THE WORK: We write your editorial unless you *want* to. If we write it, or edit your copy, you have final OK."

Among customers listed by the Taylors as having bought or written editorials distributed by U.S. Press since June 1, 1951, are some of the leading corporations in the country, plus such lobbying or special interest groups as the American Bankers Association, American Cotton Manufacturers Institute, American Legion, American Petroleum Institute, Bookmailer, Bourbon Institute, National Association of Manufacturers, and the Right to Work Committee.

Messages paid for or written by such groups go out under the masthead of U.S. Press Association, Inc., and typically are picked up by about two hundred papers, each release run as the local paper's own opinion, usually on its editorial page. Mr. Taylor says he never told the newspaper who paid for the editorial and this makes for an interesting guessing game. One mailing by U.S. Press, for example, included an editorial vigorously backing the railroad position in favor of enforced arbitration of its dispute with railroad unions. It called on Congress to make "arbitration compulsory." U.S. Press lists the Association of American Railroads as a paying client.

Other editorials in the same mailing:

1. Urged readers to watch a particular TV comedy program, noting that the hero gets the hilarious point of the plot "as will every viewer who has ever heard of a Purolator filter. . . ." (U.S. Press lists Purolator as a client.)

2. Praised the steel industry and said it was incorrect to assume that the price of steel is rising. (Among clients listed by U.S. Press are American Iron and Steel Institute, and United States Steel.)

3. Plugged Barry Goldwater and Brigadier General Bonner Fellers, head of the isolationist right-wing group For America.

Much of U.S. Press had been so fervently pro-Goldwater for so long that it was natural for it to print zealous pieces about their man before the Republican convention, though it is not evident who paid for them. Taylor said he took no money from political parties. In the usual accompanying editorial note to the July 14 mailing, just before the 1964 Republican convention, U.S. Press editor Taylor quoted a favorite source, Admiral Ben Moreell, chairman of the ultraconservative Americans for Constitutional Action, denouncing Governor William Scranton of Pennsylvania as "this brash young man." This was lavish praise compared to the quoted descriptions of the Johnson administration: " 'umbrella-squad' of native appeasers, peace-at-any-price champions [and] 'better red than dead' zealots." The paid-for editorials regularly boosted Goldwater and attacked his opponents. On July 7 an editorial said the anti-Goldwater forces in the GOP were trying to nominate a "moderate (the new word for left wing)." It ascribed this conspiracy to "Governor Scranton, backed up by his mysterious and affluent backer-uppers." In the same mailing there was another pro-Goldwater editorial, entitled "The Scranton 'Image' " (Mr. Taylor likes interior quotes as well as Capital Letters). Leaden with heavy sarcasm, it described Scranton as "a governor of some eastern state, Pennsylvania, we believe . . . the man whom Dr. Milton Eisenhower (that's the General's eastern brother) will be explaining to the Convention. . . ." (Mr. Taylor, who seems to dislike things eastern, lives and works in McLean, Virginia, a suburb of Washington, D.C., "Out Where the West Begins.")

Some of U.S. Press's editorials written by or for foreign clients came to the attention of Senator J. William Fulbright when he investigated the action of foreign agents in 1963. U.S. Press, for example, carried fervent pro-Trujillo articles paid for with Dominican money while Rafael Trujillo was dictator.

Readers who believed their local papers were being fed paid propaganda by one of the cruelest personal tyrannies in the West. These readers, vote for vote, usually have more influence on their local congressman than do urban readers subscribing to larger, less venial papers.

In 1961, U.S. Press Association received $175 from the American public relations firm Selvage & Lee, which, acting for Portuguese principals to defend Portuguese colonial policy in Africa, hired U.S. Press to send out an editorial called "How to Woo the Communists." When Mr. Taylor was told by Senator Fulbright that Selvage & Lee had received—for expenses and fees—in excess of $250,000 for its Portuguese propagandizing, the elderly man looked shocked. "I think our fees are too low," he said.

Mr. Taylor told Senator Fulbright he was paid by the Netherlands government to run an editorial praising the character of a visiting Dutch princess. "I did not meet her, unfortunately," Mr. Taylor said, "but I believe I was telling the truth." Mr. Taylor looked relieved when a senator said he had met the princess and she seemed to be a nice girl. Later, the editor of U.S. Press told me: "I never send out anything I do not think is good for the United States or that I think is not so." Senator Fulbright obviously took a dim view of U.S. Press's editorial activities on behalf of unnamed clients. (Possibly the Senator was stung by Taylor's casual disclosure that Fulbright's own family paper in Fayetteville, Arkansas, had used U.S. Press editorials.) How, the Senator asked, could a local editor know that a paid propagandist, Selvage & Lee, had written the pro-Portuguese editorial?

"I think you are disparaging the judgment and keenness of the great American newspaper editor," Mr. Taylor said.

"I just want to say I don't see how you can possibly expect them to know that this editorial was written by Selvage & Lee," the Senator insisted.

"I don't intend for them to know that, frankly," Taylor replied.

Samuel Bledsoe, a Selvage & Lee official, sounded more realistic when he said: "I think it is pretty well known to anybody who is not naïve that some interest is paying for it."

Naïve or not, the newspaper editor who receives such free editorials would have to be extraordinarily dense not to know that it was subsidized ax-grinding. While it is not unknown for a newspaper editor to be extraordinarily dense, it is more likely that he recognizes the press agentry but doesn't care because it is a cheap and agreeable way to fill space.

The result is that almost any private citizen or special group can buy his way into the editorial columns of smaller papers with relative ease and low cost. In the process the reader loses his major protector against manipulated news—the professional journalist.

If you were a reader of the *Uniontown* (Pennsylvania) *Independent,* a weekly of about two thousand circulation, you would have seen, on April 18, 1963, a column called "About Your Health." It seemed to be a syndicated news feature with a standing logotype of a silhouetted microscope. The author was Dr. R. I. Schattner, whose picture appeared in the text. The subject for the day was "Vacant Smiles," in which Dr. Schattner wrote that 22 million Americans are "without a single natural tooth" and that the major cause of this toothlessness is gum disease and the major cause of that is tartar. "However," the good doctor wrote, "tartar can be coped with. . . . During treatment, Chloraseptic Mouthwash is an excellent topical anesthetic for controlling soreness in these tender gum conditions. This non-presciptive medication also may be used as an antiseptic to maintain good oral hygiene."

It is no derogation of Chloraseptic Mouthwash (which has received admiring clinical reports) to report that at the time it was owned by Dr. Schattner, who had invented, promoted and was selling it. Dr. Schattner is an intelligent, ambitious and engaging man, a resident of Washington, D.C., who sees the public relations–news syndrome in American newspapering far more clearly than do many practitioners and professors of journalism. His column on "Vacant Smiles" appeared in about two hundred papers, thanks to a strictly cash arrangement. Dr. Schattner told me:

I paid a commercial artist about twenty-five dollars to draw that microscope logotype and then I paid Derus Media Service in Chicago a little under three hundred dollars to distribute the whole thing in mat form to eighteen hundred weeklies and dailies. We checked placement by using a clipping service: Two hundred papers picked it up. It cost me three hundred dollars. If I had run it as an ad in the same papers, I figure it would have cost at least ten times as much. But as a health column or as news, it isn't advertising, which would offend some professional codes, and it's much more effective.

A short time later the *Wall Street Journal* reported that Dr. Schattner sold Chloraseptic Mouthwash to Norwich Pharmacal Company for more than $4 million.

Large newspapers are not safe from this flood of unfiltered propaganda. Their own processing of news and editorials is usually more professional, and while the public relations syndicates get through with successful penetrations from time to time, the mechanical use of canned material tends to be limited in the metropolitan press to special pages like women's, finance, travel and real estate. The great, gorgeous photographs of cottage cheese delight or tuna fish pizza that are the standardized centerpieces for household pages are provided free by the companies selling the goods in the picture. If it is a color photograph, it is almost certain that the food company provided the expensive color separations. The glowing travel articles in some of the greatest papers show up word for word—all taken from a publicity release—in still other otherwise great papers. In such papers, the chief difference from small papers—other than the concentration in special sections—is that the photos and text are engraved and typeset by the local newspaper, rather than being reproduced from mats. Big papers usually have unions which reject the use of mats.

For the earnest, openhearted believer in the editor as the unsleeping guardian of every inch of news and editorial space, it is a shock to look at the scrapbooks of clippings compiled by the public relations firms. The scrapbooks are important to the process. Some cynics insist that the canned editorials and commercial pluggery have little effect on sales or persuasion and that their chief function is to fill the scrapbooks, which the public relations operators then show the clients as proof that they ought to continue.

This explains why most of this press agentry is plainly marked for those who know what to look for. In many photographs and cartoon features there is a symbol printed in a corner. "K," for example, means Central Feature News, which distributes free cartoons and food pictures; it also uses a small "f" for its printed features. "MS" appears on material from Master Syndicate, which has distributed, noncommittally, Medicare, AFL-CIO and pro-Nixon copy. "Z" is for Editors Syndicate, "G" for Precis, "FM" for Fred Morris Associates, and so forth. The symbol serves as a signal to the commercial clipping services which daily scan every paper in the country and compile the clippings for scrapbooks by which the syndicates and PR men keep score. There are times when an ideological point would be stronger if the lobbying group kept its name out of the canned editorial, but it is often put in nonetheless so that the clipping service reader can pick up the key words when the time comes to see how well the distribution worked.

It may be that commercial pluggery is relatively ineffective except for convincing the propagandists themselves. But it is hard to dismiss it all. Even if the charge were true, it would put the newspapers in the position of giving away what they ought to sell—advertising space. More important, such irresponsible editing helps destroy in the minds of both the advertisers and the readers the crucial distinction by which the American press lives—the difference between news and advertising.

The political effect of canned right-wing messages is not easily measured. For one thing, they appear mostly in rural areas which tend to be conservative anyway. And undoubtedly, most editors who put such material in their papers agree with it; perhaps, left to their own devices, they would write the same kind of pieces. But there is a profound difference between the identical NAM editorial appearing in six hundred newspapers and six hundred local editors thinking and writing about what the NAM has to say. The effect of the canned editorial is to make more rigid what is already a limited political and intellectual environment and to inhibit the individualistic responses which defenders of the rural life say they value.

Because rural papers have a disproportionate political impact and because they happen to be the major carriers of canned opinion, we are confronted with a perverse rule: *The smaller the newspaper, the greater its relative influence in national politics.*

There are 435 congressional districts in the country, and 203 of these, 46 percent, are rural districts. Our population is at least 70 percent urban. In many of these rural congressional districts the leading paper is a small one; in 106 of them the leading paper has less than ten thousand circulation. In twelve of them the only paper is a weekly. To imply that a small circulation automatically means surrender to boiler plate is unfair to a number of small dailies and weeklies which, whatever their politics, are plainly the product of diligent personal editorship, and precisely in those places where this takes courage because the editor does literally have to face his readers on the street. But no one can look at the common run of small papers —and at the collected right-wing opinion which they mechanically reproduce—without being appalled at the standarized puffery that floods the countryside.

The member of Congress almost never ignores what the small papers in his district say. For one thing, he may be interested in what the editor thinks is important. For another, he wants to know what is going into his constituents' heads. It is irrelevant to the congressman that the editorial may be a canned one written by a paid propagandist in New York or Chicago or Indianapolis. He knows that, whoever paid for it or wrote it, when it appears in a leading paper in his district it has helped establish the political norm among his constituents.

So behold the small-town editor. He may be a conscientious journalist and community leader who thinks out issues for himself and writes what he thinks. Let the record show—futilely, no doubt—that this writer knows such men exist; some of his best friends are creative and courageous small-town editors. But beware that the grass-roots winnower of great issues may not be the thinking editorial mind but the circling editorial hand, feeling in the lower drawer for the bit of prefabricated politics and pluggery that happens to fit, in inches and ideology, that sacred interstice for which all newspaperdom is supposed to exist: the space between the ads.

II

THE CONGLOMERATE

DISCOVERS JOURNALISM

6   News as a Byproduct

\#

Anyone who reports out of Washington has to develop a taste for mimeograph paper and its usual cargo of agency English, an aberration of the native tongue combining the styles of the Victorian novel and real estate deeds.

One day in 1967 the diurnal tonnage of government paper included one innocent-looking specimen of 176 pages, printed single space on both sides, labeled: "Federal Communications Commission . . . ABC-ITT MERGER PROCEEDINGS." Most of it abandoned the patois of the bureaucracies to raise the issue of corporate conflict of interest in journalism.

In fact, 1967 saw an extraordinary crop of government actions involving the business operations of the press. The Department of Justice obtained a consent decree against the Lindsay-Schaub newspaper chain, which it had accused of violating antitrust law by cutting ad rates, taking an intentional $3 million loss between 1956 and 1963 in an attempt to swamp a competitor in Champaign-Urbana, Illinois. The department said the chain offset its loss by profits from its other papers, just one of which, an A.M.-P.M. twin in Decatur, Illinois, with less than 65,000 combined circulation, made more than $5 million during the same period.

The Antitrust Division of the Justice Department obtained this decree while waiting for a final judgment in its Tucson case, where it had accused two one-time daily competitors of illegal collusion. During the same cherry-blossom period it began trial on its charge that the *Los Angeles Times*'s acquisition of a $1.5 million paper in San Bernardino violated the law. (Tucson won; *Los Angeles Times* lost.)

There continued private murmurs in the Department of Justice asking whether the syndicate business violates antitrust law by selling wide-area exclusive rights in popular features to big papers, to the disadvantage of the small ones.

During this same period there was dropped into the Senate hopper S.1312, a bill of sweeping exemptions of newspaper mergers and joint operations from all antitrust action if one of the newspaper parties "appears unlikely to remain or become a financially sound publication." It thoughtfully vacated all past convictions. Even the lobbyists who got through the Bank Merger Act, the most sweeping exemption in history, looked upon S.1312 with respect. The bill was cosponsored by fifteen prestigious senators of all ideological shades, whose chief bond was that they all come from states with papers in joint operations that could be affected by the Tucson case.

The important issue in the organization of journalism is not business monopoly or giantism in itself, though it presents vexing problems, all the more complicated because the press has an obvious right to protect its business interests. The central issue is how monopoly influences the flow of independent news and commentary.

This takes on overtones of geometry and geology. There are mergers that are horizontal—that is, a marriage of direct competitors, as when the *New York Journal-American* joined the *World-Telegram*; and mergers that are vertical—consolidation of firms involved in different stages of an operation, as when the *New York Times* bought a half-interest in a paper mill in Kapuskasing, Canada. There was also mention of conglomerates ("that which is heaped together in a mass or compacted from various sources"), the common control of largely unrelated businesses. For example, the parent company of the *Los Angeles Times* has twenty wholly owned subsidiaries that do a variety of things, such as printing local telephone directories, manufacturing goods, operating in real estate, selling Bibles and publishing the *Times*.

Such talk gained added meaning when the Supreme Court in the Procter & Gamble–Clorox case made it plain that antitrust action may be applied to conglomerates even when no direct competitors are involved. (A key argument by the Court was the advantage giants like P&G have in newspaper discounts to big advertisers, a point reported blandly if at all in most papers.)

All of these actions defied two of the more solemn pieties among publishers.

One piety is that news companies are under constant siege by hostile government agencies using every possible device to bring the press to heel. The fact is that government in all its branches is more hesitant to apply restraints against corporate transgressions of the press than it is against any other segment of the American economy. It would be nice to think that this comes from a delicate regard for the First Amendment. But there is a broad area of antitrust, anti-monopoly, postal and tax law that is applicable without infringement of the First Amendment; yet the press is traditionally permitted to go farther and is reprimanded more gently about corporate transgressions than are other enterprises.

The second piety is that the news apparatus is not influenced by its profitmaking activities, including advertisers. It is. Romantics continue to insist that the press is somehow corrupt for making a profit at all, which is to misunderstand a source of the strength of the American press. Another stereotype sees the advertiser as a censor of all the news, which, at least in the printed press, is not true. But this does not mean that there are no serious problems in corporate influence on the news. The reaction of dailies, magazines and broadcasting to news seriously damaging to tobacco, automobile and pharmaceutical industries, but plainly in the public interest to see, are good examples. In no such case was there an absolute or permanent blackout. But in each case the level of verification and of public concern had to be higher for these profit-sensitive news subjects than it was for other news. In the Spring 1967 *Journalism Quarterly,* David R. Bowers of Texas A & M found in a survey that publishers most often intervened in newsroom decisions "in areas which conceivably might affect the revenue of the newspaper directly or indirectly" and that they did this more than they did "in social issues such as politics, race, labor or war. . . ." The incidence of such influence in broadcasting is so epidemic that advertisers regard control or choice of content as a "right."

Conflict of interest in journalism has almost always been concerned with the individual reporter and editor, where the problems are, admittedly, real enough. In one issue of the *Bulletin* of the American Society of Newspaper Editors, a number of editors debated about political reporters who get involved in politics, sometimes for pay. Ed A. Fitzhugh of the *Arizona Gazette* said: "Moonlighting for politicians is taboo; it smacks too much of clandestine support for cash. No matter how you rationalize it, in both the public eye and in the eye of the employing politician, the newsman *does* represent the paper." It is the only sound approach to reportorial independence and public confidence in that independence; not enough reporters and editors resist moonlighting, which compromises it. Employers ought to pay their men enough and then insist they take no pay from possible news sources.

Then what about corporate moonlighting? The reporter who trims his stories to favor his nonjournalistic interest corrupts his own work. The owner of a press organization who does it corrupts an entire institution. If enough institutions are influenced by the same pressures, then the entire body of public knowledge and social values is distorted.

This is what made the 176 pieces of mimeographed paper from the FCC such a pregnant package. The first twenty-two pages consisted of an order by a majority of the FCC permitting the biggest broadcast merger in history, between International Telephone and Telegraph Corporation and the American Broadcasting Company (or, technically, allowing transfer of ABC's seventeen stations to ITT; the FCC has no jurisdiction over who owns the network but the seventeen wholly owned stations are crucial to the deal).

The remaining pages were devoted to the dissenting opinions of three commissioners; 118 of them were from Commissioner Nicholas Johnson.

For a time, this Johnson was the most noticeable man of that name in Washington. A young lawyer in the hell-raising tradition, he asked irreligious questions in simple declarative English and his dissent was primarily responsible for reopening the case (and for the ultimate dissolution of the merger deal).

Among Johnson's reasons for rejecting the merger was ITT's deep financial involvement in areas which ABC News would have to report. ITT has commitments in forty countries and its officers have said that they protect these interests by obtaining sympathetic policies in Washington.

Johnson wrote: "Chile, Peru, Brazil or India might someday wish to nationalize the telephone companies which ITT now owns in whole or in part. It has happened to ITT in the past and could easily happen again. ABC News and public affairs personnel would have to comment on the affair at length. If one admits the possibility that such nationalizations could be put in a favorable light, the potential for conflict with ITT's economic interest is obvious."

What would happen, he asked, if a rebel movement in Brazil got sympathetic treatment in an ABC news documentary that the government of Brazil tried to block? "The added leverage which the government of Brazil could exert because of ITT's Brazilian holdings would be substantial."

ITT gets 40 percent of its domestic revenues from defense and space contracts. What if ABC wanted to criticize the high rate of this spending?

Johnson asked: "Are we to accept . . . that although ITT may continue to exert pressure as an advertiser on the programming of CBS and NBC, it will exert none as an owner on the programming of ABC?"

This last worry was sharpened on April 20, 1967, when reporters for the *New York Times*, AP and UPI were subpoenaed to testify on ITT's alleged "extraordinary" efforts to influence news about the merger hearings. Eileen Shanahan of the *Times* testified that ITT's senior vice-president for public relations made "accusatory and nasty" remarks about her stories and asked her "if I didn't feel a responsibility to the shareholders who might lose money as a result of what I wrote." ABC drove the point home by having its affiliates ask members of Congress in their districts to support the merger. It was a dull politician who didn't wonder if his access to constituents through broadcasting wasn't at stake.

Though aggressive and inept pressure is nothing novel in news coverage, it does raise the interesting question of what can happen when a reporter or editor is pressured not by an outside force but by his own employer. Or by an outside force with financial influence, as when complaints about some UPI wording in its ITT-ABC stories brought out that ABC pays UPI $250,000 a year for various services.

The issues raised by Commissioner Johnson cast light on the ITT-ABC type of conglomeration that already exists with NBC and CBS.

NBC is owned by Radio Corporation of America, which also has substantial foreign investments (one subsidiary alone, NBC Enterprises, operates in ninety-three countries), is the leading international telegraph company, owns RCA Victor records, Random House books, a drug company (Hoffman-LaRoche) and a car rental firm (Hertz). (ITT owns Avis.)

CBS, according to filings at the Securities and Exchange Commission, has thirty-nine major subsidiaries, fifteen of them in foreign countries, owns Columbia Records, and Fender Musical Instruments. It told stockholders in 1965 that it was working to increase its defense and space orders. It owns no car rental service but SEC records show that in 1965 CBS invested $21 million in the credit affiliates of General Motors, Ford and Chrysler. At one annual meeting, for example, it reported increased investment in toys and the acquisition of book publisher Holt, Rinehart and Winston, and denied plans to merge with yet another publisher.

Although diversification and conglomeration create problems of economic power, the central concern here is with the impact on news when it is controlled by corporations with deep nonjournalistic financial involvement. We are seeing a shift from journalism companies that moonlight in other work to conventional businesses that happen to moonlight in journalism.

It is a problem looked at only spasmodically, as when a Fred Friendly quits his network. Or when competitors complain that RCA color television gets special breaks on NBC. Or when CBS is suspected of firing a sports announcer because he said unkind things about the CBS subsidiary, the New York Yankees.

Specific stories influenced by specific business interests cannot tell the whole story. Each network and most publications can point to individual productions detrimental to their business investments. Most of them reject outright bribery or crass coercion. One of the greatest exposés of all time was the *New York Times*'s destruction of Boss

Tweed's gang, accomplished after the publisher, George Jones, in 1871, turned down an offer of $5 million to suppress the stories. This was pretty crude. Today a syndicate of lawyers and brokers could use the money to get control of a corporation to buy an offending news medium, not just knock out one series of articles.

There have always been ingenious ways to buy influence in the news. Just before World War II the Japanese government secretly took over control of a respected hundred-year-old journal, *The Living Age*, in which it planted stories. It created a newsletter that went to every American editor. It bought silent interests in *Current History*, *North American Review* and the *Saturday Review of Literature*.

Such successful transactions are not at the heart of the conflict-of-interest problem. It is true of individual reporters and just as true of their employers that the worst corruption is self-imposed; the expedient, profitable or comforting bias is rationalized as news.

For more than fifteen years after 1911, the elder Hearst used all his communications agencies to provoke a war between Mexico and the United States. His papers ran such headlines as: MEXICO PREPARES FOR WAR WITH U.S. He owned the International Film Service, which made films about Mexican plots to overthrow the American government. In the 1920s he ran in all Hearst papers a spectacular series based on documents showing that Mexico had bribed four United States senators with $1,115,000.

Most Hearst readers had no way of knowing that the Hearst family owned 2,500 square miles of Mexican mines, timber, chicle and ranches that were threatened with government seizure.

When the bribery of the senators was investigated it turned out to be untrue; the documents Hearst had paid for were primitive fakes. The *New York Herald Tribune* for January 7, 1928, quoted a Treasury Department handwriting expert: "Anybody who would pass a consideration for these documents must have been in a very acceptable mood."

Most of Hearst's biographers, including W. A. Swanberg, think that when he printed them Hearst honestly believed the documents to be genuine. That is the point: he suffered the human tendency to be "in a very acceptable mood" about anything that supported his private interests.

Newspapers and magazines have these moods. They are generous in their coverage of anti-billboard activities. They seldom muckrake their leading advertisers, such as department stores or car dealers. Most reporters and editors know that the system is "in a very acceptable mood" about news that favors the system's financial interests.

Only occasionally do the more explicit influences come to the surface. During the 1964 presidential campaign the fiercely pro-Goldwater *Manchester* (New Hampshire) *Union-Leader* delivered an astonishing rebuke to Goldwater for criticizing Jimmy Hoffa. It turned out that the Teamsters had $2 million in the *Union-Leader*. Joseph Kennedy put $500,000 into the ailing *Boston Post* at about the time the paper switched its support to John Kennedy.

Monopoly in communications decreases the chances that an interested party will notice and call attention to corporate conflicts in the news. The Hederman papers in Jackson, Mississippi, have done incalculable harm to their state by incitement of destruction and malice and they have also been accused of serving the owners' non-journalistic investments. Their last competition ended five years ago.

The Wilmington, Delaware, papers belong to the Du Ponts and have been used to protect company and family interests. The *Houston Chronicle* and *Post* are also handmaidens of the ruling oligarchy, which controls much of downtown Houston. In both Wilmington and Houston the distortions to favor owners' interests became known only after tough editors quit or were fired.

But competition is hardly a guarantee of mutual monitoring on the corporate level. There is competition for ads, circulation and even news in Houston, Chicago, Los Angeles and San Francisco, but it stops short of the executive suites.

Owners frequently respond explosively to questions about corporate conflict in the news. This could be because an owner is truly disinterested, or that he twists the news focus but in such a way that it seems reality to him. Or he could be thinking of the virtuous as typical of the whole trade. There are publishers and there are publishers. One owner of a daily in a Florida city owned substantial real estate in the town and sold it to avoid any possibility of inhibiting his paper's freedom, and those who know this can point to it as proof of incorruptibility. But there was also a publisher in Connecticut who owned real estate in his city, most of it substandard, and fired a new city editor who ordered an investigation of slums. There are relatively few news staffs that cannot—privately—tell variations on this theme.

The crux of the issue is not the specific bias. It lies in the fact that journalism is more important today than at any time in the past. The human race is better educated and equipped with more efficient communications. Dynamic interaction—in communities, in the country, throughout the world—is in response to some kind of communication, usually journalistic. If this communication does not reflect reality as rigorously as trained and independent professionals produce it, then the consequences can be profound, and already have been. More than ever journalism not only needs to be accurate but has to be looking at the most important issues.

The ultimate question in corporate conflict of interest in the news is whether news and commentary as a whole would be different if news corporations had no outside financial interests. And if different, whether it could come closer than it does today to the needed improvement in reporting and relevant commentary. The resolutions of most urgent issues—war and peace, the growing chasm between rich nations and poor, decay of cities, inadequacy of schools, race relations, contamination of environment—depend on allocation of national wealth, which means both social policy and taxes. If the news and its interpretation are increasingly merely a byproduct of huge corporations whose primary concern must be conventional gain, then this is not a minor matter in public information or in the development of social and fiscal policies.

Nevertheless, diversification and conglomerates seem destined to grow.

In the process more news operations will become appendages to conventional businesses. It is not illegal to include news in a conglomerate. One long-term remedy would be the development of professionalism, the strengthening of the tradition that puts a wall between front office and newsroom.

Another could be to inform the public of any news organization's outside financial interests, which might restrain corporate interference with news and at least notify the consumer. Something like this is required of all companies traded on the stock market, but relatively few newspapers and broadcasting stations are openly traded. Systematic and locally available reports of this kind would be therapeutic. Publisher opposition would be not much more than 99 percent, and since universal disclosure of press finances would require an act of Congress, it may be necessary to wait for an act of God.

The "Independent" Newspapers
of the Du Ponts

———

\#

The Wilmington, Delaware, newspapers, the *Morning News* and the *Evening Journal,* are, according to a standing editorial masthead, "independent" newspapers. A formal resolution issued by their owners on April 13, 1936, and presumably still in force, instructs the editors that the policy of the paper is, among other things, to "avoid blind partisanship . . . never to misrepresent the facts either in their news or editorial columns; never to resort to suppression except for the public good . . . always to give all sides a fair hearing on all public questions."

In this the two papers are no different from hundreds of others across the United States that also call themselves "independent" and solemnly declare that their owners insist on editorial freedom and want no fiddling with the news. As in Wilmington, the owners don't really mean it, or else the words mean one thing to editors and something else to owners.

Behind the flag-draped mastheads, in the real world of the newsroom and board room, the news is fiddled with by management, either crudely through direct intervention or more subtly by picking editors who know what is expected of them. The owners aren't always as big as the Du Ponts or as heavy-handed, but it would be better if they were. What happened with the Du Ponts in 1964 has happened since in other places without the explosions.

At the time, Creed Black, an intense Kentuckian, was thirty-nine years old, with editorial experience on *Stars and Stripes*, the *Chicago Sun*, the *Chicago Herald-American*, the *Nashville Tennessean* and the *Savannah News-Press*. He seldom turned his back on a controversy ("I don't mind a fight") and until June 1, 1964, was vice-president and executive editor of the two Wilmington dailies.

Black's departure from Wilmington was not unusual in the tribulations of the trade—it was an enactment of a ritual that goes on through American newspaperdom with all the unhappy regularity of Aztec sacrifices. For what Creed Black did overtly goes on silently and secretly in editorial offices and board rooms all over the country, in election years more than ever.

The owner of the two Wilmington papers is the Du Pont Company, which is to Delaware what God is to Heaven. More precisely, the owner is the Christiana Securities Company, a holding company that is to Du Pont what the church is to God. Christiana was formed in pre-World-War I days to buy out a faction of Du Ponts during a bitter family feud. It owned 27 percent of the Du Pont Company and all the stock of the News-Journal Company, which, with the exception of a paper of 13,600 circulation in Dover, publishes the only dailies in Delaware.

The Du Pont Company is run by an executive committee of nine men, called the ExComm. The Du Pont family interest in the company and other concerns is exercised through Christiana, whose ruling group has some seats in ExComm. There is a single room on the ninth floor of the Du Pont Building in Wilmington in which the secretary of Christiana can cast one ballot to constitute a "stockholders' meeting" of the News-Journal Company.

The News-Journal Company had a board of directors of ten men. In 1964, four were working executives of the paper, including Creed Black and the papers' president and editor, Charles L. Reese, Jr., son of the Du Pont chemist who led the company's research to international stature in World War I. There were two "outside men," that is, non-Du Pont: Ralph K. Gottshall, president of Atlas Chemicals, once a Du Pont firm, spun off after antitrust action but still in friendly symbiosis with its parent; and J. J. B. Fulenwider, vice-president of Hercules Powder, another former Du Pont firm separated by antitrust order, with 300,000 of its shares now owned by Christiana. A seventh member of the board was Robert H. Richards, Jr., counsel for the paper, a director of the Du Pont bank, the Wilmington Trust, until recently Republican National Committeeman from Delaware, and son of the legal genius who created Delaware's friendly corporation laws and guided the formation of Christiana.

The three ownership directors were Henry Silliman, son-in-law of Irénée Du Pont; Robert R. M. Carpenter, Jr., known as Bobby, nephew of the president of Christiana, himself on the board of Christiana and owner of the Philadelphia Phillies baseball team; and Henry B. Du Pont, president and patriarch of Christiana and until recently vice-president of ExComm. H. B. Du Pont was the ruling man in the ownership, with Carpenter increasingly influential.

The Du Ponts and the press have had a long joint history. The family first appeared in the Delaware press on January 1, 1806, when one of the papers in town (Wilmington then had a population of 3,500 and two newspapers; it now has a population of 100,000 and two newspapers) carried a grocery store ad for smoked herring, Old Peach brandy and "DuPont & Co's. gunpowder." Since that time their printed presence has been more dramatic. Like any normal family, they have no love for adverse publicity, but their wealth and power have given them more than their share of it. It is a huge family, with about 1,600 contemporary members, 250 of them important in the empire and a handful of them potent leaders. It is a large but close-knit group.

For the last seventy-five years the news has often been intolerable for the Du Ponts, since their prominence made their most embarrassing private moments terribly public. These moments were plentiful, with family scandals and fights, suicides, bordello shootings, spectacular intra-family marriages and divorces (HE MARRIED A BARMAID, a *Chicago Daily News* headline said of a Du Pont on November 12, 1889), and senatorial investigations of the "munitions lobby" in the 1930s. All of this gave the family good reason to fear the press.

Alfred I. Du Pont saved the company for the family, and helped plunge it into the newspaper business. After most of the clan had voted to sell out to their closest competitor, Alfred formed a troika of leadership in 1902 with his cousins, T. Coleman Du Pont and

Pierre S. Du Pont (with the help of Pierre's ingenious assistant, John Jacob Raskob). The three cousins took over the $24 million enterprise with a total cash outlay of $2,100—the incorporation fees.

The newspaper appendix to the Du Pont anatomy was acquired after the family declared war on Alfred, not so much because of his spectacular divorce and remarriage to his divorced cousin but because of his flamboyant announcement of it in the *Wilmington Morning News*. When he got back from his honeymoon, Coleman told him: "Al, now you've done it," and said he should get out of the company. Alfred refused and the fight was on, Alfred on one side with about one-fifth of the clan, and Coleman and Pierre on the other, with the bulk of the family. The feud involved politics; Coleman had ambitions to be a senator or even President. Alfred started a new bank and deliberately made his building two stories higher than the twelve-story Du Pont Building one block away.

Henry A. Du Pont, on Coleman's side, bought the *Wilmington Evening Journal*. In response, Alfred bought the *Wilmington Morning News* and six downstate papers and there followed a journalistic firefight that shredded state politics, the company and the family. When Coleman's political drive collapsed, Alfred ran a headline in his paper:

BANG! T. C. DU PONT'S BOOM BLOWS UP!

The explosive figure of speech was considered unforgivable bad taste in a family that lived (and sometimes died) by gunpowder.

When Alfred got his second divorce in 1906, nothing appeared in any Wilmington paper, but there was a full account in the Philadelphia papers, an enduring pattern that continues to this day on sensitive Du Pont family or Du Pont Company news.

World War I made the company what it is today, but the postwar depression caught Alfred personally $10 million in debt. He sold out his share of the company and the *News* to his family enemy, Pierre. The same faction of the family then took control of the company and of every daily paper in the state.

Over the years the family shaped itself by shrewd decision and careful selection of in-laws to govern the company in a more orderly fashion, ruthlessly weeding out incompetent members from company leadership in the most discriminating nepotism in the country. The

Wilmington newspapers were only afterthoughts in this process and they settled down to conventionality and drab dignity.

In 1960 the executive editor, Fendall Yerxa, left to return to the *New York Herald Tribune* and a management consultant firm combed the country for an acceptable professional to take his place. They came across Black, who was ready to leave Savannah. The *Morning News* and *Journal—Every Evening* (as it was then called) were not very different from most papers: the owners insisted that within certain principles agreed upon beforehand, the editors were free to put out the best product they could.

Two other prominent American newspaper editors took a look and decided not to take a chance. One of them asked what would happen if he decided to endorse a Democrat. When he was told that this would be a decision for the board of directors he said good-bye and went to the nearest hotel and "got stiff." On the other hand, previous editors had not found the job intolerable and Reese, the president and editor, is a respected man in the trade. Black took the job.

The technical history thereafter was comforting. Their names were simplified to *News* and *Journal*. The typography was reformed; one paper had looked like the prewar *Herald Tribune* and the other like the postwar *Baltimore Sun*. Some of the old content (SANDWICHES ON MENU and MASONIC CLUB AIDE TO SPEAK) disappeared to make room for harder news from new bureaus. An inbred staff was leavened with younger talent selected from other papers and from universities. In four years the combined morning and evening circulation went from 106,000 to 125,000. The 1963 revenue and profit were up 25 percent to the highest level in the papers' history. What was more significant, the old picture of the Wilmington papers as Du Pont Company house organs began to fade. Younger editors even asked if the Du Ponts still owned the paper.

Despite professional appearances, inside troubles had begun in 1961. The starting point was "Operation Abolition," the House Un-American Activities Committee film that was used as a set propaganda piece for right-wing causes. The Delaware State Police were showing the film under official auspices to schoolchildren, churches and civic clubs. The paper editorialized against the official showings of a factually dubious piece of work as dangerous precedent for political indoctrination by the police.

This stand brought severe pressures from the owners. An Un-American Activities Committee staff member and the narrator of the film, Fulton Lewis III, was a guest at the home of H. B. Du Pont, where the papers were severely criticized by a group made up largely of right-wing Delawareans. The film later was shown at a program sponsored by Mrs. H. B. Du Pont and Robert Carpenter.

H. B. Du Pont ordered the papers not to comment editorially on the film. Instead, for two months the news columns carried attacks against the paper by the state police chief. The letters columns printed criticisms of the papers and the patriotism of the staff. The editors themselves were ordered to remain silent. The owners' old resolutions —never to resort to suppression and always to give all sides a fair hearing—were invoked by the editors, in vain.

At about this time the papers provoked the disapproval of the president of the University of Delaware, an institution close to the Du Ponts, who served on its board of trustees. The dispute seemed to be over the reporting of campus controversies, which the university regarded as bias on the part of the dailies. H. B. Du Pont ordered the papers to suppress a number of items involving the university.

It was at this point that Bobby Carpenter, a nephew of H. B. Du Pont, was placed on the board. It was plain that the papers were being enlisted in a passionate conservative crusade. From this time on there was growing acrimony between the editors and the owners.

In 1962 the editors proposed that they interview major candidates for state office from both parties to help them editorialize during the campaign. This was approved. But when the editors decided to back the Democratic candidate for Congress as "the lesser of two evils," there was a special meeting of the board of Christiana Securities. Christiana is probably the richest investment trust in the world, with assets of more than $3 billion, but that day its attention was directed to the cosmic subject of an editorial that compared the demerits of two candidates for Congress and came out begrudgingly in favor of the Democrat. Christiana had the editorial rewritten outside the newspaper office. It finally appeared, watered down from the original. The papers did endorse one Democrat openly—the candidate for state auditor.

Other clashes came quickly. When Shell Oil wanted to build a refinery in Delaware, the owners ordered the papers to stop comment on the issue. When Congress was considering legislation for relief of the Du Ponts in selling their General Motors stock under court order, the papers were told not to criticize Senator Byrd, chairman of the Senate Finance Committee. During the same period, the Du Pont Company public relations department asked the paper not to run on page one a statement on the matter by Harris McDowell, Democratic member of Congress from Delaware, for fear it would anger a friendly senator.

H. B. Du Pont also told the paper to put the damper on stories of public charges of mismanagement at the Wilmington airport, whose chief activity is handling the business of a private aviation corporation in which H. B. Du Pont has an interest.

Some idea of the clash between owner ideologies and professional practices can be seen in the complaints of board members. The significance of these conflicts is not so much in the views of the owners (who, of course, have views, as do all interested citizens) as it is a revelation of what happens when an owner fails to understand the role of the monopoly newspaper and the discipline of news.

Henry Silliman and Robert Richards, both members of the paper's board, formally requested through Richards that the paper give a prominent play to a family wedding. "I do not know if this is in accordance with your policy or would require a deviation from your rules. If the latter is true, there should be exceptions to every rule. . . ."

At a time when Richards was on the paper's board and also Republican National Committeeman from Delaware, he complained bitterly to the editors that the paper's reporter had written a conventional news account of a Democratic rally when he should have turned it into a pro-Republican essay. Richards even wrote his own anti-Democratic story as an example of how the paper should have carried it, though presumably he was not at the rally himself. "This was a matter which, if properly handled, could, in my opinion, have been very useful to the Republican Party and their success at the polls in November," he wrote.

When Wilmington began having racial troubles, H. B. Du Pont told his editors: "A continual overplaying of integration in our papers certainly plays right into the hands of the radical element of our population . . . many of the writers on your staff seem to have a degree of dedication to certain causes which would make them appear to be quite far to the left."

Most revealing is the collection of complaints issued by Carpenter to the executive editor.

On an editorial praising President Kennedy's Supreme Court appointments: "Why should we devote space to one who is an enemy of private enterprise and the capitalistic system?"

When editors asked him if his complaints about their comments on a bill by Representative McDowell meant the paper should oppose everything McDowell was for, the answer was: "I would say, Yes."

When an editorial criticized some Republican choices of candidates: "Are we endorsing the Democratic Party by criticizing the Republican Conventions? . . . Could we not become a house organ for the conservative cause?"

When he objected to running a letter to the editor signed by sixty-four University of Delaware students favoring integration, the editors asked if they should close the column to all letters from students. His answer was: "Yes."

On an editorial noting that French Socialists had outmaneuvered French Communists: "Should the *News-Journal* take the position of favoring actions of any Socialist Party? I believe it is a grave error for a subsidiary of Du Pont to follow the philosophy of the ultra-liberal whose objectives are destruction of capitalistic systems."

It is apparent in retrospect that two conflicting developments had occurred. The Wilmington papers, as with most metropolitan dailies in this country, were in fact broadening their professional and social scope. This was in line with the growing sophistication of the overwhelmingly Democratic or moderate Republican urban audience. At the same time, the owners seemed increasingly rigid in their demands for ultraconservative orthodoxy and family convenience, in both news columns and editorials.

With the 1964 election campaign approaching, and with Senator Barry Goldwater involved, it was obvious to the editors that something had to be done to resolve these conflicts. The editors pressed the owners for a statement of what they expected of the papers, some mandate that could be followed. When the editors suggested that the papers be committed to the Republican cause with editorials to "focus on an objective appraisal of the chances of the various candidates," H. B. Du Pont objected that this idea would "leave editorial writers free to snipe at candidates for the Republican nomination for President."

Black asked mostly for consistency. In a memo noting that he had received orders from four or five separate owners plus the public relations department of the Du Pont Company, he asked: "How many bosses are we expected to please and take orders from?" (He had, for example, run the names of large holders of General Motors stock, as released to the national press by the Du Pont Company public relations office, and had received bitter castigation from two members of the Du Pont family.)

On May 19, 1964, the owners of the Wilmington *News* and *Journal* gave their answer. They said that Charles M. Hackett, executive assistant in the public relations department of the Du Pont Company, would be the boss of news and editorial operations of the papers, with Black serving under him. Black quit. The day before, the announcement was made that the Wilmington papers had won five of fifteen possible first prizes in a publishers' association judging of papers in Pennsylvania and Delaware.

The ending followed tradition. Black wanted to publish his letter of resignation, which said, in part: "I, for one, need no further evidence that the ownership wants the *Morning News* and the *Evening Journal* operated as house organs instead of as newspapers." H. B. Du Pont vetoed the idea. After the first edition of May 19, carrying simply the news of his resignation, Black posted his letter on the newsroom bulletin board and the Philadelphia papers printed it before Wilmington did.

H. B. Du Pont, at the time, denied Black's assertion and said the newspapers "have never been and never will be operated as a house organ for any organization. Christiana Securities Corporation reaffirms their determination that the News-Journal Newspapers be operated independently with the objective of being a constructive influence in the community, in the state, and in the nation."

Efforts to obtain further comment from the papers' management during the preparation of this article were unsuccessful. H. B. Du Pont was unavailable for comment. Robert Carpenter, when asked about his role in requesting changes in the newspapers' content, said:

"I wouldn't want to comment on the subject." Charles L. Reese, Jr., president and editor of the newspapers, also declined to discuss it.

The most depressing aspect of the Wilmington episode is that it is not unusual. Few families are so powerful, organized or dominant in their state as are the Du Ponts, but newspaperdom is filled with owners whose assumptions of their responsibilities are based on their non-newspaper businesses and whose journalistic enterprises are peripheral to both their personal experience and their daily attention. Unlike the McCormicks and the Ochses, such owners do not have to live with the day-to-day consequences of their decisions, nor face constituents whose information and opinions they oversee.

Decisionmaking in newspapers has a fundamental difference from that of most enterprises. Success in conventional business has a simple measure: survival and profitmaking. Both are essential to newspapers, but a paper that only survives and only shows a profit can be a failure as a newspaper. The newspaper is a community educational institution run for profit. The owner's relationship to the news he prints is something like a university trustee's relationship to reading material selected for courses.

There are hundreds of dailies in which editorials on certain subjects are as predictable as a catechism, whose news departments are designed to overreact or underreact to certain kinds of news, notably financial and political, not because of incompetence or sensationalism but because of the impulse to create a picture closer to the dreams of the ownership. Nor is it unusual for owners to believe that their papers' staffs are filled with radicals dangerous to the point of doubtful patriotism. Owners, typically, are conservative Republicans, and staffs—in journalism, as in most professional fields—tend to be Democrats.

If there were a tradition within newspapering to contain this distrust and tension between owners and staff, as there is in universities, it could result in a pluralism with the advantage of a checks-and-balances system. But there is no such tradition. Too many owners have been alienated too long from the social realities their staffs must perceive and report (and amid which the staff lives and owners generally do not). The *Boston Transcript* was perhaps the last metropolitan daily that lived within a closed elite. The power of both the *Transcript* and its elite was changed with the Depression. Millions of words in thousands of editorials will not bring back the mid-twenties.

There are continual legislative and vigilante attacks on freedom of the press. It will be an uncomfortable time when the owners of newspapers have to depend for preservation of this freedom on the understanding of constituents with whom the owners have been out of sympathy and, worse, out of touch for thirty years.

When Creed Black resigned he got the unexpected sympathy of some prominent citizens of Delaware, partly because not many hired hands publicly dispute the Du Ponts. Some publishers wrote him that owners will never learn. Editors sympathized with him. And one bright university student who had planned a newspaper career wrote:

"I have always had a few doubts about the newspaper business . . . if this is at all typical of the behind-the-scenes actions in the fourth estate, I'll have no part of it."

8   Houston Listens to the
            Ghost of Jesse Jones

———

\#

Among the most fervent declarations about American institutions are public testaments to the need for freedom of the press, and no one pronounces these with more passion than the press itself. From standing mottoes on page one, in prose and poetry across editorial pages and in unrelenting rhetoric from publishers' conventions comes the message: the democratic process is founded on the rock of free and independent newspapers.

Most of these proclamations imply the danger of control by government. Some suggest other threats, from welfare statism to public apathy. Over the years, among the most insistent alarmists of the internal threat to freedom has been the *Houston Chronicle,* the largest paper in Texas and at one time the property of Jesse Jones. But in the past decade the greatest contribution the *Houston Chronicle* made to the maintenance of native American institutions was to conduct a continuing and depressing demonstration of how not to operate a free paper in a free society, and to remind its brethren in the trade that the most immediate threat to a free press in this country is their own conflict of interest.

In the 1950s the *Chronicle* was an unabashed mouthpiece for the city's aging oligarchy, dull, jingoistic, reactionary and falling behind its competitors. Brought in to rejuvenate the paper in 1960 was William P. Steven, a professional editor (moderate Republican) who reversed the paper's dying tendencies and looked at the *Chronicle* as though it were being published for the whole community. In addition to this heresy, he was pretty radical: he supported higher education, Lyndon Johnson and civil rights. So he was fired by the oligarchy. It was the most spectacular story in American newspapering that week in September of 1965, reported by all major Texas dailies, the wire services and national news magazines. But in the *Chronicle*'s account of the change—the conservative team of the 1950s was put back in charge—Steven's name did not appear, and he became an unperson in the manner of fallen political gods in the Soviet encyclopedia. The paper began shifting back to the right.

Three months later the oligarchs agreed to sell the *Chronicle* to the Houston oil millionaire John Mecom as part of an $85 million package that included hotels, banks, office buildings and a laundry. The deal would change the commercial power structure of the sixth largest city in the country, but the *Chronicle*'s bland story was one-eighth as long as the one in the opposition *Post*. After Mecom moved in, the paper continued its rightward shift and changed largely by playing up its new proprietor's interest in oil and in horse and automobile racing, and by providing spectacular coverage of his daughter's wedding.

The Mecom deal collapsed, and the *Chronicle* reverted to the oligarchy, along with the laundry. The *Chronicle* did not report that the deal had been canceled, let alone why, presumably on the grounds that it was none of the public's business. Readers were not even told that they had lost a newspaper proprietor. Mecom's name, like Steven's before him, was merely dropped from the masthead and replaced by that of Jesse Jones, who had been dead ten years. If Houstonians depended on their biggest paper, they would not know that their community had undergone a profound change, even though the paper was part of that change. And they would not know that their leading newspaper, the most prominent Texas representative of that crucial institution of a free and independent press, was being bought and sold like an anonymous link in a string of corporate hot dogs.

Among the depressing morals to be drawn from the turbulence in Houston is the reminder that the American press has hardly begun to think about, let alone solve, a fundamental problem of conflict of interest. The press has been vigorous about pointing to conflict of interest among politicians, occasionally exposing men and agencies in government who let private profit interfere with their public duty. Newspapers were particularly noticeable stressing the horrors of conflict of interest and payola in broadcasting. At infrequent times a few papers will even expose individual reporters or editors who compromise their reportorial objectivity by taking money, favors or glory from news sources. But they have been virtually silent about a major source of conflict of interest in journalism: the danger that the publisher of a local paper will have a financial interest in an enterprise that should be reported objectively but is not.

For example, the group that controlled the *Chronicle* in 1965 also controlled a large bank in town, whose bitter stockholder struggle was reported in the *Wall Street Journal* and on page one of the opposition *Post,* but never mentioned in the *Chronicle.*

So it was typical that when the *Chronicle* was sold in December, along with the same large bank and downtown real estate, Houstonians depending solely on the *Chronicle* would have known nothing of the event unless they had caught the final edition of the December 6 paper, and even there they would have been limited to a twelve-and-a-half-inch story. Six months later, when it was "unsold," the readers were told nothing. The *Post* had three chaste paragraphs forty-eight hours later.

The *Post* has not always compensated for the deficiencies of the *Chronicle.* It cooperated, for example, in keeping out of print in Houston the name and fate of the discharged Steven. Competition does not necessarily produce good newspapers. There are too many cities where it seems to produce the opposite—Boston and San Francisco—and a number of places where monopolies print good newspapers—Louisville and Saint Petersburg. Competition merely increases the odds that news will be printed and public questions asked and investigated. There is no longer competition in 97 percent of American cities with papers, and in the remaining 3 percent the tide of monopoly seems to move on inexorably, as it has in Houston in recent times.

Until 1964 there had been three papers in the city. For years the best one was Oveta Culp Hobby's morning *Post,* staid, occasionally enterprising, but never as vigorous or as authoritative as one would expect from the only morning paper in the country's sixth largest city, remarkably rich. There were two afternoon papers. The Scripps-Howard *Press*, a wretched product, was a flamboyant, superficial jab in the civic rib cage. The other was the *Chronicle*, reactionary and stingy with the news, for years the voice of its early owner, Jesse Jones, and after his death, of his fiscal trustees.

In 1960 the *Press* had a circulation of 102,000. The *Post*, with 218,000 circulation and the only staff exhibiting signs of metropolitan-caliber ability, grew slowly to dominance in the city. The *Chronicle* had a circulation of 205,000, but it was out of sympathy and out of touch with large segments of the community. John T. Jones, Jr., the titular head of the *Chronicle*, decided it was time for a change. Jones, the favorite nephew of Jesse Jones, is tall, slender, slow-speaking, with a facial resemblance to his uncle except for a contemplative quality.

John Jones decided to change the *Chronicle* to a paper for a modern metropolis, which Houston desperately needed. For years the city had been racked by ideological wars of the most primitive kind, most dramatically in its educational system. The schools were dominated by citizens who regarded sympathetic mention of the United Nations in the classroom as Communist indoctrination, who considered racial integration an alien plot, and who eschewed such forms of federal aid as school lunches but grasped it in the form of federally supported military training for high school boys.

Jones's instrument for the awakening of the *Chronicle* was William P. Steven, a man of heavy build and hearty voice, with a national reputation for rejuvenating newspapers. He had started out in his native Wisconsin, had edited in Tulsa and had enlivened the Minneapolis news scene. He is of that breed of newspapermen who possess instinctive rapport with their generation, a drive to go where the action is and an immunity from the contagion of bureaucracy and ultrarespectability.

Like his friend Lyndon Johnson, Steven is a calculating plunger. (Years ago he told a *Time* magazine reporter that his editing philosophy is "Plan now, print later," but it came out in *Time* as "Print now, plan later" and continues unchangeable in the corridors of *Time* as a famous Steven quote.) He parted with the Cowles management in Minneapolis largely because young John Cowles had risen to the point of editorial leadership, and a good newspaper can stand only one leader at a time. It is typical of Steven's shrewd enthusiasm that he found his next job by compiling a list of all the papers in the country with three characteristics: big enough to pay him a good salary, dull and with an editor over sixty. There were eight. In each case he arranged for a friend who knew the owners to let the publisher know Steven was a good man and available. One of the papers was the *Chronicle*.

In September 1960 John Jones and Steven spent a day and a half talking in a room of the Rice Hotel in Houston. Jones wanted Steven to do for the *Chronicle* what he had done for papers in Tulsa and Minneapolis, make them interesting and make them grow. The two men liked each other. As they approached a decision, Steven told Jones: "You know, John, there is one thing that troubles me about working in the South that you ought to know. I feel that integration is an essential fact in the demonstration of democracy. I think it is necessary for the full development of the economy. And I think it is the only way to make our foreign policy mean anything in a world of mostly dark skins. Outside of that, I have no strong feelings on the matter."

As Steven remembers it, Jones replied: "The *Chronicle* supports the law of the land. The only trouble I'll have with you is that you may want to talk about it too much."

The *Chronicle* stopped being dull and archaic. Emphasis moved from columnists of the far right, like Paul Harvey and Fulton Lewis, Jr., to those of the center, like James Reston and Max Freedman. The paper subscribed to the *Los Angeles Times–Washington Post* wire service and the *New York Times* news service (after the *Times* service appeared, conservatives in town began calling the *Chronicle* their *Pravda*).

Almost at once Steven began building up the local news staff, which was suffering from inbreeding, age and malnutrition. Top reporters were getting $120 a week, and he raised their salaries to $165. He attracted bright young journalists from outside the paper. One photographer, Ted Rozumalski, became the only man ever to be named twice as national Photographer of the Year. Reporter William Porterfield won an Ernie Pyle Award in 1963. Saul Friedman was named a Nieman Fellow at Harvard. The staff began doing series of articles on urgent local problems, among them sympathetic accounts of the nature of racial relations in the city (there are 300,000 blacks in a city of a million). Much attention was devoted to the need for faster development of higher education. The *Chronicle* withdrew its support from the conservatives on the school board, pressed for televising the school board proceedings against the bitter opposition of conservatives, and won.

Steven spent money, but he also saved some. For years it had cost the paper $100,000 to publish a 6 A.M. edition merely to get an extra 7,000 circulation in the fight against the *Post*. Steven scrapped that edition. In 1964 the *Press* finally gave up and sold its assets to the *Chronicle*, which then became the largest paper in Texas, with 254,000 circulation.

The opposition *Post* began to perk up. It brought down William Woestendick from the highly successful Long Island *Newsday*, and its national and foreign news improved. The changes were long overdue in a city with four universities (total enrollment 25,000), a large petrochemical and shipping community with global rather than parochial interests, and the huge NASA space center.

For the first time, urgent issues could be discussed openly without destructive recrimination. The pre-Steven *Chronicle* spoke for the financial lords of the territory and their eccentric politics, and everyone knew it; the most dangerous political radicalism it had entertained was to support Governor John Connally, even though he was, in a manner of speaking, a Democrat.

A man who lived and worked in Houston during the Steven period said: "You have no idea what difference it made that the *Chronicle* changed. It wasn't dangerous to be a Johnson Democrat anymore, or to support minority groups, or speak in favor of Medicare. Before, if you supported these things, they made you feel like the village crazy man."

The nature of this change is implied in the award given Steven in October 1964 by the Houston chapter of the American Jewish Committee "in recognition of his constructive and effective labors in guiding the Houston *Chronicle* toward accomplishing the information of our populace and the improvement of opinion in Houston."

It was typical of the new role of the paper that on September 2, 1965, Steven and his counterpart on the *Post*, William Hobby, Jr., spent much of the day conferring with Houston Mayor Louie Welch over an alarming local development. It was during the Watts rebellion in Los Angeles, and though Houston blacks showed no sign of hostility, hysterical whites had bought out all the guns in a number of stores and were mounting armed patrols of neighborhoods. Steven put in continual calls for his boss, John Jones, and for his managing editor, Everett Collier, but, oddly, could not reach either one.

Steven arrived home tired and worried, but his wife, Lucy, alert and articulate, insisted that he shake his concern and join a family celebration. It was a gay evening. But by eleven-thirty Bill and Lucy were in bed reading when John Jones called and said that he was coming right up. Bill assumed that Jones wanted to talk about the racial tension.

Just before midnight, Mr. and Mrs. Jones arrived at the Steven home, in the fashionable southwest of Houston. Bill and Lucy were in bathrobes and over an initial drink made friendly small talk. Then Jones blurted out: "This is the hardest thing I ever had to do. Bill, they had a meeting today, and they got you."

As Bill and Lucy Steven reconstruct it, the conversation went like this:

STEVEN: Who is "they"? And what do you mean, they got me?
JONES: You know. The Endowment.
LUCY: Who?
JONES: The trustees.
LUCY: What do you mean, they got Bill?
JONES: You're all through, Bill.
LUCY: Why? Why?

There was no direct answer. Much later that night, Jones said: "Bill, you had a vision. They don't want a vision; they want a voice."

The Endowment is The Houston Endowment, Inc., a tax-free charitable foundation started by Jesse Jones in 1937 with a gift of $1,050,000. Jesse Jones, banking, lumber and real estate millionaire and a government administrator under Herbert Hoover and Franklin Roosevelt, died in 1956. Ten years later his Endowment calculated its assets at $168 million. Others think it was $400 million, but no outside audit has ever been made.

Under the law, the Endowment existed solely to support charities. But its primary impact on the community was as a powerful, tightly held corporate empire. It had an important interest in thirty-two corporations, a majority interest in twenty-five, including half a dozen banks, three hotels, several downtown office buildings, real estate and the Mayfair House hotel on Park Avenue in New York. Through its communications properties it was the major controller of political and social intelligence in the city of Houston. At the start of the counterrevolution that swept Bill Steven out of his job, the tax-free foundation owned 100 percent of KTRH Broadcasting Company, a major station in the city, 31 percent of a local television station and 100 percent of the *Houston Chronicle*.

From 1951 to 1964 the Endowment had an income of $97 million and gave $19 million in charity. When Representative Wright Patman of Texas began investigating abuses by some tax-free foundations, the Internal Revenue Service momentarily revoked the Endowment's foundation status but later restored it.

Four men and one woman controlled probably the largest single corporate force in the city. John Jones used to be a sixth trustee and chairman of the board, but he resigned in order, he said, to buy $3 million worth of broadcasting properties from the Endowment without conflict of interest. The remaining five trustees were all related to Jesse Jones by blood, marriage or former business association. They were J. Howard Creekmore, president, a former bank employee of Jones's; Mrs. Audrey Jones Beck, granddaughter of Jesse; John Beck, her husband; J. Hurt Garrett, a former employee of Jones's and senior vice-president of the Texas National Bank of Commerce, second largest bank in the city, controlled by the Endowment; and W. W. Moore, former associate of Jesse Jones's, president of Bankers Mortgage Company, a holding company owned 97 percent by the Endowment.

There is special irony in the episode. Reformers of newspapers have long dreamed of ownership by a foundation that would be immune to commercial attitudes and pressures. But as it unfolded in Houston, foundation ownership produced a list of almost every pitfall in business domination. This does not necessarily negate the idea of foundation support, but it would seem to for foundations run by men who are essentially corporate administrators with control of operating businesses. For example, the *Chronicle* represented only one-twentieth of the Endowment's total assets. Even if the newspaper never showed a profit, this would be tolerable to the total economy of the foundation. It served the trustees instead to have the paper protect the property and politics of its owners and do it more effectively by overwhelming its competing papers, which it did by consistently cutting its advertising rates secretly for big advertisers, keeping its monthly subscription rate abnormally low, running exorbitant editions to help put one competitor out of business and dominate another. The owners of the *Chronicle* had another convenience: they held notes for some time on the owners of their competitor, the *Post*.

The chief evil of the Endowment's ownership is the same as that of any business conglomerate possessing a newspaper: the paper is always in danger of becoming a means to the parent corporation's nonjournalistic ends, a handmaiden rather than a detached reporter.

A second danger is that such ownership is ideological. A man who controls a dozen nonjournalistic businesses usually has nothing in his experience telling him he is obliged to make his property available to the ideas of others. The owners of the *Chronicle* seemed to find any such notion of obligation intolerable, and Steven insists he was fired because of that intolerance. "The conservatives won," he says.

As he cleaned out his desk, Steven got a call from President Johnson, who wanted to know what was going on. "Mr. President," Steven said, "we carried every precinct but the right one." He meant that the paper had support from the community but not from the board room of The Houston Endowment in the Bankers Mortgage Building. It was from here that the counterrevolution was mounted. First the foundation trustees dissolved the board of the *Chronicle*, which had included Steven, replacing him with their new editor, Everett Collier, who had been a columnist during the paper's reactionary period in the 1950s. Then they loaded the paper's board with members of the foundation board—Creekmore, Garrett, Moore and John Beck.

Jones seems to have been a powerless witness to the wreckage of his paper. He has said that he was told to take it or leave it.

There was almost unanimous indignation among the new hierarchy at reports that internal politics had anything to do with the firing. I tried to ask all the trustees, but most of them were unapproachable.

The receptionist for Mr. Moore at Bankers Mortgage brought back the message: "He knows what you want, and he won't see you." But I found the number two man on the board less bashful. J. Hurt Garrett had his office on the executive third floor of the Endowment's Texas National Bank of Commerce (the biggest bank it controls). He was an elderly jowl-faced man reminiscent of overseers in New England textile mills.

"We didn't like their editorial policy, that's all," he said. "They had everyone up in arms. Nobody liked it. I never heard anything but complaints about it. . . . It was all this racial desegregation business. Things were all right in Houston before they came down. But all this racial business—nobody liked it. And I don't like all this Johnson stuff, and all his civil rights, too. I know that Jones and Steven are friends of Johnson, but all we got was complaints about the paper's policy on that."

Mr. Garrett sounded quite credible. When he said of the paper's policy, "Nobody liked it," presumably he meant nobody on the third floor of the Texas National Bank of Commerce. Two-thirds of Harris County voted for Lyndon Johnson in 1964. And when he said he heard nothing but complaints, this, too, sounded plausible. My guess is he did not subscribe to a Houston weekly called the *Forward Times*, which went mostly to the black community, and which ran almost a full-page editorial on the firing of Bill Steven, saying:

A strong positive force that has quietly but effectively gone about the business of helping Houston Negro citizens move up into new heights of dignity and opportunity has been fired from his position.

Not many Negroes were personally acquainted with William P. Stevens [The *Forward Times* made a common error of putting a terminal *s* on the name], but most were well aware of the fact that for the last four years the Houston *Chronicle* had shifted from a staunchly conservative newspaper to one that openly advocated school integration and printed editorials that warmed the heart of the depressed and disadvantaged.

What the Negro citizens did not know was the man responsible for all this change was William P. Stevens, backed by John T. Jones, Jr. What they may not have realized recently, when a front-page announcement was run in the *Chronicle* announcing that a new editor had been hired was that the old editor, William P. Stevens, had been fired. . . . It is an ominous warning of things to come or to say the least it is an indication of the end of a short, short era.

The editorial referred to the possibility that people in Houston might not know that Steven had been fired. On September 3 the *Chronicle* ran a large story on page one on the new appointments but omitted any mention of Steven, and of the Endowment, which made the changes. Over at the *Post*, a story about the firing was prepared but killed by the top brass.

So the news of Steven's discharge had to travel by underground: two church newsletters (one said "truly disturbing," another "a tragic mistake"), two weeklies (the *Forward Times* and the conservative *Tribune,* which ran a straightforward news story). Later someone mailed out thousands of reproductions of stories in national papers and news magazines on a sheet entitled "News all over the U.S. but not in Houston."

Suppression was traditional at the *Chronicle*. When a columnist mentioned in print that there was a plan to study a downtown air terminal, the head of the Endowment, Howard Creekmore, personally called the paper in anger. The Endowment also owned the Rice Hotel, where most of the airlines have their offices. A new downtown terminal was not encouraged in the *Chronicle*.

But the Houston Endowment had been under pursuit by the Department of the Treasury and by Congressman Patman. Patman was digging deeper into the Endowment in the summer and fall of 1965, compiling an impressive record, only partly publicized at the time, of the Endowment's large-scale corporate dealings and its modest indulgence in charity. Patman proposed and even the conservative Treasury agreed that there ought to be a law limiting the right of tax-free foundations to control operating businesses.

During this period the foundation was looking for a suitable buyer, Steven was fired and Creekmore decided that John Mecom was the man to buy the *Chronicle*. Why did they pick him?

Collier's explanation is: "The trustees of Houston Endowment were determined to keep these properties in the hands of someone who has the same deep love of this community and the same concepts for its betterment and progress that Jesse Jones had." The trustees no doubt felt they were expressing "the same concepts for its betterment and progress" when they fired Steven for being too liberal, pro-black and too militant a reporter of the town.

Mecom was pro-Johnson in a Texas sort of way, but he was not an ideologue. He maintained an office in the *Chronicle* and ran the same kind of paper the post-Steven editors did under the Endowment. The paper remained to the right of the Steven paper. Three months after Mecom took over, its columnists on domestic affairs were William White, Henry J. Taylor, Raymond Moley, Les Carpenter, Marianne Means, Victor Reisel, William Buckley, James Reston, Max Freedman and David Lawrence. Four of these (White, Freedman, Carpenter and Means) were close friends of Lyndon Johnson's. The only nonconservative among the remainder was Reston, and he appeared less frequently than before. Liberal cartoonist Herblock no longer appeared. The paper dropped Ralph McGill and Whitney Young, and conservative columnist David Lawrence was run twice as often as before.

Almost a year after Steven was fired, a series of articles on the black community, criticizing among others the slum landlords, had not been published. Reporter Saul Friedman, who later went to Detroit, had worked on the series four months. It was ready for publication when Steven was discharged.

On a number of urgent local issues the editorial page went blank. It decided, in an abrupt change, that the televising of school board sessions was not important. When Attorney General Nicholas Katzenbach made a major speech urging the city to complete its racial integration willingly and without rancor, the *Chronicle*, whose editorials under Steven had not been reticent about giving opinions, merely suggested that readers look at the speech. Another editorial recommended that readers look at a certain column of William White's. An editor told a subordinate: "That will be a signal to President Johnson that we're still with him." The new *Chronicle* apparently hoped to send esoteric signals to the President that would go undetected by the owners and the readers.

When the Houston Endowment fired Steven, an indignant citizen of Houston wrote to the White House: "The time has come to license newspapers—to assure that they will use their licenses for the benefit of the public and not just for special interests."

Licensing of the press is unconstitutional and unwise. But newspapers ought to worry about how often the idea appeals to a frustrated public. There is almost nothing a community can do about a local paper that fails in its primary duty. Starting a new metropolitan competitor is too much like a man dissatisfied with his automobile trying to start a new General Motors. He might have done it fifty years ago but not today. Nor is there any effective way he can reach owners who choose to remain unresponsive.

The country's newspaper proprietors, the vast majority enjoying a monopoly, preside over an institution that should be the most sensitive detector of change in society. But among major American institutions, newspapers have been the least responsive to upheavals in civilization since World War II. Government, education, religion and much of corporate enterprise have adapted to altered conditions in economic and social life, but newspaper owners have clung to the past. They seem to be reminded of their special status under the First Amendment only when someone suggests changes in the second-class mailing privilege or the payment of standard wages to delivery boys. Their response to the notion of the press being accountable to the public is to bar reporters from sessions of the American Newspaper Publishers Association. In addition, the dangers of news monopoly are increasing.

Newspapers have generally supported the idea that policymaking federal officials should disclose their financial holdings and sell those that might conceivably tempt them to influence their work for their own benefit. The American newspaper is almost a branch of public administration. It is the most important single instrument of information in a society peculiarly dependent upon public knowledge and public opinion; for its own future and the national good it needs to be as free as possible, and it needs to assure increasingly dubious readers that it is free.

III

THE PRESIDENT

AND THE PRESS

#

Washington tourists looking into the Smithsonian Institution's Museum of History and Technology can see a great steam locomotive of the Southern Railway mounted on rails inside the building. The giant machine, 188 tons and ninety-two feet long, had to be set in place before the walls were constructed and is now a permanent captive inside the air-conditioned museum.

Three blocks from the new museum is the White House, which, in the 180 years since its cornerstone was laid, has similarly grown up around the great engine of American politics, the President, enshrining him and at the same time symbolizing his inability to reach the outside environment directly.

The President, after all, has little face-to-face contact with most citizens. A leader of 200 million people spread over 3.5 million square miles can bring his personality to bear at first hand on only a microscopic fragment of the electorate—a limitation felt by the first President even though he led a nation of only 4 million people on one-fourth of our present acreage.

George Washington, like Presidents after him, appeared to the public largely through the newspapers. Like many other Presidents, he came to regard the press at its best as an imperfect instrument and at its worst as a curse upon the people. Leaders typically expect the press to be an unswerving ally in what the leaders conceive to be noble purposes; when instead newspapers extract, compress and mix the leaders' messages with antimessages from their enemies, it seems outrageous adulteration; when papers are antagonistic it seems close to subversion. George Washington had an overwhelmingly sympathetic press. Yet when he retired he was so enraged at the small but noisy opposition that among his first acts as a private citizen was cancellation of newspaper subscriptions (an act of retribution to which a President may still resort).

Frank Luther Mott, historian of the American press, has shown that it is not unusual for Presidents to have a majority of newspapers against them. Among those elected over majority press opposition were Jefferson, Madison, John Quincy Adams, Jackson, Van Buren, Polk, Pierce, Lincoln, Hayes, Garfield, Benjamin Harrison, Wilson, Franklin D. Roosevelt, Truman and Kennedy. Yet Mott's conclusion, made some years ago, that this is a manageable fixture of American politics may need a new look. Of thirty-seven presidential campaigns up to 1936, only three reveal winning candidates with less than 40 percent of editorial support (Jefferson, 33 percent; Van Buren, 35 percent; Lincoln, first campaign, 30 percent). But since the New Deal, the percentage of papers and circulation in favor of Democratic presidential candidates has been running consistently so low as to place the daily press in a fixed position in the political spectrum. Franklin Roosevelt in 1936 had 26 percent (by circulation) in his favor; in 1940, 23 percent; in 1944, 18 percent; Truman in 1948, 10 percent; Stevenson in 1952, 11 percent, and in 1956, 15 percent; Kennedy in 1960, 16 percent.

Many papers opposing a President as a candidate later support him on specific issues, but in general the percentages represent a line of ideological separation. Modern opposition papers, unlike those in the eighteenth and nineteenth centuries, have a tradition of keeping editorial opinion apart from news. But the rigidity even of labeled opinion that has prevailed for the last thirty years still presents severe problems for any Democratic President. For one thing, the newspaper field is now institutionalized so that editorial opinions, even those out of touch with contemporary values, will not suffer local printed competition. It costs too much to start rival papers and existing dailies are supported for reasons other than their opinions. Further, the division of opinion is a crucial one in domestic matters, since newspapers generally throw their editorial lot on the side of business in any conflict with labor or government or consumer, and these conflicts are among the commanding issues at home. Finally, though there is substantial divorcement of editorial opinion from ordinary news, there is still a discernible and often important difference in treatment of news among pro-Republican and pro-Democratic papers —differences in reaction time to certain kinds of news, differences in emphasis and differences in the initiative taken on reporting.

Any modern President who finds himself in conflict with the industrial or financial community can take it for granted that a vast majority of the press will be against him. Further, if the conflict is sufficiently prolonged, this opposition will make a difference in the outcome. While the press has not demonstrated that it can change the minds of people who have strong feelings on matters directly affecting them, the emphasis of the news and the nature of its display can affect that part of the political landscape brought to the attention of the reader.

The clash between President Kennedy and the steel companies in 1962 may have been a milestone in the presidential use of communications. The milestone is symbolic only, for a change has been on the way for more than a generation. But since then it has been clear that new communications are effective. President Kennedy, certain of massive newspaper opposition to his pressures to force steel companies to back down on their price increases, reached over the heads of the press in one dramatic television presentation. This so placed steel on the defensive and stimulated public opinion that it permitted his other moves against the companies—investigations by the Department of Justice, a Federal Trade Commission inquiry, FBI calls, hints of new legislation—a chance to prevail, which they did.

In the five-minute opening statement of his live television press conference on April 11, 1962, President Kennedy demolished the opposition—before the 319 correspondents had even left the auditorium. This was the culmination of a generation of worry by Democratic Presidents over the editorial attitudes of the daily press. Franklin Roosevelt began using radio systematically in his first Fireside Chat, March 12, 1933, eight days after his inauguration, chiefly to impart a sense of confidence and leadership to a dispirited people. But it was not long before he began seeing it as an instrument for reaching over the press, which became increasingly hostile. His press conferences were still informal affairs in his office, with no quotation of the President permitted. While Roosevelt exploited the conferences for his own purposes, he also came to regard them as baiting sessions between him and the publishers, with the correspondents as intermediaries.

Radio, on the other hand, was a clear channel from the White House into the voter's living room. But Roosevelt was chary of striking too hard. "I am purposely avoiding use of the air because to use it at the controversial stage of a controversial legislative body spells more controversy" he wrote to Colonel Edward M. House in 1934. (Four years later FDR praised U.S. Steel during a Fireside Chat: "Today a great steel company announced a reduction in prices with a view to stimulating business recovery, and I was gratified to know that this reduction involved no wage cut." The next day U.S. Steel aimed a statement at Roosevelt saying it was by no means committed to keeping up wages and making it plain that the President deserved no credit for the price cut. *Plus ça change.*) By 1941 Roosevelt so clearly saw radio as a countermeasure to newspapers that he worried over how many newspapers owned radio stations. World War II suspended further development of radio as a President's domestic weapon. With peace came Truman, whose use of radio made some difference, but who lacked the force of Roosevelt.

Television represented a quantum lead in the means available to a President to bypass the printed page. Yet, curiously, it took more than a decade of mass television before a President used it at its maximum power to win a particular battle. Political television started in the fifties, during which Eisenhower, a nonpolitical President, did not make a strong impression on the medium, except to project his personal qualities of earnestness and sincerity. Senator McCarthy and his antagonists, however, dramatized the political power of television. Cameras launched Adlai Stevenson at the 1952 convention and John Kennedy in the Nixon-Kennedy debates in 1960. But these were public events pressed home by an impersonal medium, not an impersonal medium commandeered for his own use by a President.

Before April 11, President Kennedy was interesting but not potent on television. He was impressive at his television press conferences

not so much for what he said as for what he did not say, for his careful selection of words, for his irony. He seldom galvanized an audience. His was the passive voice, the subjunctive mood, the noncom-
mittal adjective. "It would be inappropriate to comment . . ." or "I
found the talks—ah—useful. . . ." He may have been moved by
several influences: a natural reserve in public; a sensitivity to his close
election; a desire to maintain a nonpartisan official stature; a commit-
ment to fighting hard in private and letting his enemies save face in
public. During personal confrontations he showed other qualities. He
seemed to have hypnotic powers over his antagonists, clutching them
to his breast and releasing them to walk glassy-eyed out of the White
House. Platoons of the opposition, like George Sokolsky, emerged
from private sessions with the President under an old-fashioned Irish
spell. But to the general public he appeared cautious, courteous and
filled with limitless capacity for conciliation. Once, at his January 24,
1962, press conference, a flash of driving toughness came out, when
he nipped a security-risk campaign in the bud, but apparently the
U.S. Steel scouts did not diagram that play back at headquarters.

At 3:31 P.M. on April 11, at his thirtieth press conference, the
President started his polemic against "a tiny handful of steel executives." There was now no prudent circumspection and no personal
reserve, but instead strong words and as fierce an emotion as John
Kennedy permitted himself on a platform. He spared nothing—
patriotism, dying soldiers and selfishness in time of peril. At three
thirty-six the battle against steel was over. Yet it would be twenty-
four minutes before the correspondents would get to their telephones
and hours before they would get into print.

The President's attack would appear in 312 morning papers the
next day, in the hands of perhaps 24 million readers. The wire services would carry most of the dramatic opening statement in their
major stories. Most papers would not carry the verbatim transcript.
The *New York Times*, the *Wall Street Journal* and the *Washington
Post* (aggregate circulation: 1.7 million) and possibly half a dozen
others would carry, as usual, a condensed text, probably about half
the total, on a subsidiary wire, as would United Press International.
(They have no way of knowing how many clients regularly use it, one
service estimating as low as six.) Practically all papers, in the disci-

pline and tradition of printed news, would carry in their stories not only the President's most dramatic words, but also those of his adversaries who would have had time to reply.

In addition, there would be the publishers' editorial reactions. In the steel case there would be an initial period of shocked hesitation and then strong opposition to the President's using any influence in wage and price determination and to the measures he used to fight the U.S. Steel increase. Some editorials would see the end of free enterprise in America and, in the televised statement, an event akin to Lenin's entry into Petrograd. The editorials would have special influence within the business community (which tends to look to them for moral support) and serve to consolidate opinion there.

But before any of this could happen, the general public, or that part of it that saw television and heard radio that same day, had an opinion, based on the words and image of the President himself in their living rooms. Television networks carried the press conference in full, live or delayed an hour, to a maximum of 8.5 million homes (ratings are vague on an unsponsored program like this). Even more effective were the evening network television shows, almost all of which used most of the videotape of the opening statement. These were seen on a maximum of 13 million sets when perhaps as many as 35 million people were watching. The radio networks fed the taped full conference to affiliates (but had no way of knowing how many took it or when they used it). Radio Press International transmitted the full conference in voice to its eighty subscribers and believes that at least twenty used it in full that same day. RPI's transmission also used four minutes of the President's voice at his conference on its news broadcasts, which most clients used.

The next day all broadcast media carried something of the press conference by Roger M. Blough, chairman of U.S. Steel, but this was less impressive, partly because the head of U.S. Steel cannot compete for attention with the head of the United States. That night the CBS television documentary "Eyewitness" reviewed the events before an audience of possibly 6 million.

The effective difference between the broadcast and the printed news was not just speed and numbers. It was in emotional impact, in the mechanical advantage of broadcasting that permits a lone man to present his own words in their full emotional context without opposing views or critical analysis.

Without any medium's wanting it to happen, television has become the President's medium. The newspapers are somebody else's medium —the reading public's, the business community's, the publisher's—as well as the President's. Neither in emotional response nor in sociological makeup are the two audiences the same. What necessarily comes across in live television and radio is what most public figures would like to see of themselves in print if they could manage it—their own words verbatim without filtration by reporters and editors, intruding comments by others or editorializing by the medium.

Many people were worried by the President's quick victory over steel—people who had no special love for U.S. Steel, but who felt that steel, for all its unlovable qualities, was outmatched. The same awesome power of the President to transmit himself electronically into the American living room could be turned on a less powerful adversary.

The newspaper tradition of presenting the other side of an argument is indispensable, though it is often resented by readers who believe that when angels speak the press should not drag in the devil for a word in reply. This is an old problem of reporters and newspapers: partisans seldom want nonpartisan reporting. This is not to say that broadcasting is without editorial balance, but that the nature of the medium usually makes the lone news source seem far more credible than he is in print. While the news source is talking, no contrary voice can be transmitted.

Newspapers now have to report an event to a public whose opinion about the event may already have been formed by another medium. This will be especially so on any issue in which the decisive impact is made by television. In one sense it is a healthy discipline on reporting, since the reader will have viewed the event and heard the words himself. But prior knowledge could be misleading—as anyone can recall who ever heard Senator McCarthy standing in front of a closed hearing room to give his interpretation of what went on inside. To the newspapers—and the later broadcast news programs—falls the burden of preventing stampedes of opinion on issues where only one side has been presented.

This burden will test the public's faith in newspapers at a poor time in the political history of the contemporary daily press. The disadvantage of the printed word is not just that it is slower, but more that there is an undercurrent of suspicion about the politics of newspapers, based on their overwhelming opposition to the mainstream of social and economic change in the United States during the last thirty years. What papers may do out of conscientious regard for the whole truth will inevitably get mixed up in the reader's mind with what papers have done in the past out of partisan politics.

Particularly on issues of family economics the press is vulnerable to attack, because since 1934 the general public has shown—through its votes and its folk sayings—its belief that in any conflict between business and the consumer, the newspapers are on the side of business. This set of mind is the Achilles heel of the daily press in American society, and every intelligent politician knows it. In a sense, this is unfair, considering the large body of honest reporting in newspapers. But public skepticism exists.

The quick television victory of the President in 1962 made it plain that newspapers are not always the most effective link between the President and the public and that any time he chooses, a commanding public figure can go over the head of the press. Implicit in this demonstration is the possibility that should the press consolidate against a President, as it has in the past, he need not be so chary as before of antagonizing the newspapers and, if need be, he can appeal to the endemic suspicions of the press's own readers.

10   From JFK to LBJ:
           From Cool to Hot

\#

Two hours after the assassination of President Kennedy, an important
official back in Washington received word from the news ticker that
a local law enforcer in Dallas was telling the press spectacular
theories about the killing, apparently unaware either of the facts or
of the awesome consequences of what he was saying. The Washington man snatched the phone on his desk and then, the phone in midair
and his face blank, he froze. Slowly he put the phone back on its
cradle. With a sad and distant expression, he told a visitor: "It's
funny, but two hours ago there was no question exactly whom I'd
call and know this would be taken care of. Now I'm not so sure."

Much of official Washington went through something like this. The
great inverted tree of power branching out from a President is often
diagrammed in civics books with cabinet departments represented by
neat squares angled into the main trunk, but the flow of real power
does not follow the official charts. It follows the private lines of personal relationships that make certain men, some with only the vaguest
titles, important sources of power, policy and information. The
stronger a President and the more acute his taste for personal management, the greater the significance of his personal relations. It is the
informal power structure that is important to reporters. When John
F. Kennedy died, his personal lines of power disappeared and new

lines came slowly into focus. For the news community of Washington there was parallel confusion and adjustment. Reporters need to know the nature and priorities of official thinking, to work on crucial points for the release of blocked information or the confirmation of hypotheses. The abrupt change in the presidency started a change in news gathering.

The changes in the personality and sources of news were further complicated by the late President's revolution in projecting the President and his ideas to the general public.

With the succession of Lyndon Johnson, there was a double paradox in presidential press relations. John Kennedy, more than any other President in history, was a genuine hobbyist on the subject of the printed press. Yet he turned to television as his primary medium. Lyndon Johnson, like most classic examples of Congressional Man, was devoted to the spoken rather than to the written word. Yet he turned back to the printed press.

John Kennedy's interest in the press was personal. Naturally, he never let his expertise go unused in solving his political problems, but there was no cynicism involved. Like most hobbyists, he spent a certain amount of time cursing the object of his addiction but he always went back to it.

Kennedy seemed to read every magazine and newspaper in sight, including the *New York Herald Tribune*, which he officially banished but always unofficially read. What he didn't read himself he learned through memoranda from his staff, and this enormous intake ranged from learned journals to popular magazines.

The chief result of the President's reputation for ingesting journals was that everyone in his power structure also read. It helps to know what the boss is thinking about, so the entire federal establishment read the *New York Times*, the *Washington Post*, the *Washington Evening Star*, *Time* and *Newsweek*, looking for things that might involve them and might have caught the President's eye. There was an unprecedented system of indirect communication with the President through the news columns. Members of Congress, journalists and private citizens were able to obtain presidential attention this way when they could not get by the White House staff.

The presidential reading had another effect. Everyone in the establishment spoke with greater restraint, because whatever they told an interviewer might get reported and be read by the President. In

Washington anything said by a political person, including what he mutters as he puts on his snow chains, can end up in print; consequently, there was remarkable unanimity of expression by the official family. Some of this was based on unanimity of ideas, but some of it came from a consciousness of the sharp eye in the White House conning the news columns or that more likely repository of candid end-of-the-evening remarks, the women's pages. The sharp eye could be followed by a sharp tongue.

The Kennedy interest was genuine and his knowledge sound. He could press Richard Rovere on details of articles in *The New Yorker* in a way no one could fake.

On another occasion, when he was flying to the Vienna conference with Khrushchev, a time hardly conducive to low-level press agentry, John Kennedy came back for a moment's relaxation with the pool correspondent on his flight. The correspondent had prepared himself for just such a lucky moment with a mental list of questions. But when Kennedy lowered himself into the seat he asked the correspondent: "Why do you suppose Bill Lawrence left the *Times*?" William H. Lawrence had just left the *New York Times* for the American Broadcasting Company, and for five minutes John Kennedy discussed the problems of a correspondent's adjustment from the typewritten to the broadcast word.

This is one reason Kennedy rang so true to so many politically hostile newspaper and magazine publishers. They couldn't resist the surefootedness of his conversations about newspapers and magazines —and the President's careful briefing about his guest's particular publication.

So what did John Kennedy do? He turned to television.

The live television press conference, held in a large auditorium, was John Kennedy's invention. So was the intimate year-end symposium with television correspondents. He did it, of course, because it was effective. The President of the United States, appearing in the nation's living rooms talking with correspondents the public had come to recognize, was almost irresistible.

Furthermore, John Kennedy was good at it. Paradoxically, he was not a spellbinder or very good at creating emotion in public. But he chose his public words with precision and prudence and this, with his grasp of essence and detail, added to that peculiar sense of loss felt with his death. There had grown subtly with the months of presidential sparring on television a feeling that he knew both what he was talking about and what he was not talking about, and that he could be trusted to understand the facts and make wise decisions. Lastly, television gave the President direct access to the public. For any Democratic President who knows that at election time or in a national fight with the business community the majority of newspapers will be against him, this was of enormous importance and John Kennedy knew it.

What did this precedent mean for a new President? Primarily, it placed an unfair burden on Lyndon Johnson to continue the press practices that were suited to the peculiar tastes and strengths of his predecessor.

Lyndon Johnson was plainly a different man and his relations with the press would be different. Like most members of Congress, Johnson talked and listened more than he read and wrote. This is not because Congress is filled with illiterates but because the job conspires to make even the most thoughtful man incapable of getting twenty minutes to sign letters, let alone write them himself. (If the laws of forgery were invoked, every key staff person on Capitol Hill would disappear into a penitentiary.) Congressional Man can't possibly absorb his avalanche of constituents' mail or the thousand bills a year he votes on. He has a staff that does that for him and then fills him in with five-minute oral briefings, often given, literally, as the boss half runs down the corridors toward the chamber for a vote. When he arrives at the chamber he obviously will have no time to read the amendments and their alterations, let alone to prepare an analysis, so he gets a fifteen-second oral fill-in by a functionary hired by his party or from a colleague. In his committees—if he has direct responsibility or personal interest—he listens to a mass of spoken words, which are later read only by correspondents and other masochists. If he has a job like Lyndon Johnson's old one in the Senate, he can no more do business with written words than could a lion tamer, and for about the same reasons.

And yet as majority leader, Johnson was required to keep sorted in his head an enormous collection of facts and figures and personal histories, ready for instant recall and lightning rejoinder. He had to depend on a quick visceral rather than a cerebral reaction. On his official missions as Vice-President he followed the same pattern, wanting to be briefed orally rather than by memoranda. His relations with the press traditionally had been personal and hortatory rather than cool and calculated. He seemed a man made for the red-eyed television camera.

So what did he do when he became President? He did not venture a televised news conference for more than two months, and then only on a reduced scale.

Some network executives were sufficiently worried to fly to Washington to urge the President to reinstate the big televised press conference. Some of the printed-word correspondents were resentful. Although they hated the cameras, as do most true believers, they missed the advance notices of the big conference. Some missed the special importance that television gave their questions. Quite aside from whatever hambone strain television brought out in the reporters, there was the real potency of having the President confronted with a question while the whole country watched, quite a different thing from a question posed in a small group with no one watching.

"We will do what comes naturally," Mr. Johnson told reporters in an informal gathering in his office soon after he became President. "Maybe it will be a meeting of this kind today; maybe a televised meeting tomorrow, with a coffee session the next day." During a period of transition when "continuity" was the byword, the new President created a pause to permit himself to find methods of news dissemination appropriate to his own tastes.

The big televised press conference under Kennedy seemed to be an irreversible step in the evolution of presidential press relations, datum zero in our time being under Calvin Coolidge. Coolidge insisted on written questions ahead of time, producing, as Tom Wicker has written, "the deadliest bores of a deadly boring era in Washington." Herbert Hoover had a reputation for productive press relations, but the great leap came with Franklin Roosevelt, who called reporters into his office to cajole, scold, joust and joke with the men who crowded around the edge of his desk. The FDR conferences reflected the special élan of that particular President but they were also the beginning of the steep curve of growth in the importance of government and the public interest in it.

Each President properly fashions his news methods to his own personality, but all of them work within a framework of the rising level of education and sophistication in the American population. The Washington press corps has grown in size and quality in response to this—by Truman's time the conference had to be moved out of the President's office into the Indian Treaty Room in the great stone pile of the Executive Building next door. Here some of the intimacy began to disappear, but men were still only a few feet from the President and the continuing inhibition on direct quotation left him somewhat relaxed. Dwight Eisenhower's press was even larger but he kept the same room, adding movie cameras, which produced the feeling of shooting a mob scene in a Victorian sardine can. The television and radio tapes were edited before release. Printed words, held back until "Thank you, Mr. President" started the foot race for the telephones, were still the prime conduit of the President's answers to the press.

When John Kennedy moved the conferences to the State Department auditorium, it seemed an inevitable concession to the great growth in numbers of correspondents and the size of the national audience. When he made the television cameras and radio microphones live, it became a public performance devoid of the safety of editing, with correspondents in the role of supporting players. Of the 1,300 correspondents accredited to the White House (more than two hundred of them foreign) from two hundred to four hundred attended the big conferences. The large numbers required a physical setting that made close personal contact impossible. The President stood on a stage and, far away, the correspondents had their questions picked up by special microphones aimed at them like machine guns. There were few follow-up questions and little continuity because it resembled a dialogue shouted over a canyon. The live cameras meant there was no retrieving an indiscreet or misconstrued remark. If television spread the President's words wider, it made them blander.

And yet it seemed—and still seems—an inevitable part of the new world of direct communication. More than any other single technique, the Kennedy press conferences gave the general public insight into the business of their government. For the first time in millions of living rooms there was some realistic hint of foreign affairs, legislative struggles and administrative problems. It all came with an element of suspense because it was a contest that was unpredictable. The whole nation (or at least 18 million viewers) watched as the President came to bat and the reporters served up curves, floaters and beanballs. For reporters, including those who never wrote of any particular conference, it was instructive to watch the President, since they knew the unstated danger in many questions and could observe the President's handling. The big televised press conference is not a precise journalistic device but it is a major accomplishment in public political education. If it did nothing else, it at least caused more newspapers to print the transcript.

Many people had accepted the Kennedy conference as an established ritual. Yet on December 18, 1963, something appeared in the official transcript of President Johnson's press conference which had not been seen for many years.

THE PRESIDENT: I guess this ought to be *off the record*. . . . I do not like to start that, but . . .

So shortly after noon on December 18 there was a sudden reversion back thirty years to the style and setting of Franklin Roosevelt.

Two weeks earlier, on a Saturday, the White House regulars had appeared for a briefing by Pierre Salinger, the presidential press secretary. They were unexpectedly swept into the President's office. "I told Pierre a little earlier in the morning I was going to buy coffee later in the day," the President told the stunned correspondents, "but I didn't really know how much coffee I was going to buy. He has more friends than I anticipated."

The immediate effect of the impromptu conference was to double the attendance at the two-a-day briefings given by the press secretary. Now there was not only a chance of seeing Pierre Salinger but of having coffee with the President. More than one editor, seeing the wire pictures of that first conference, had wanted to know why his Washington correspondent wasn't there.

The Johnson office sessions had their disadvantages. They were unannounced, otherwise four hundred men and women might show up for coffee in the President's office. There was no careful preparation of questions, as is done in the better bureaus in town for an announced conference. Correspondents who concentrate on foreign affairs and on Congress, not being squatters in the White House lobby, did not take part in the questioning.

There were differences in the quality, as well as the form, of the two Presidents' dealings with the press.

Journalism-cum-history was Kennedy's avocation. His original associations with newspapermen, largely East Coast, were more personal than political. "The Georgetown Journalists"—well-to-do newspapermen like Rowland Evans, Jr., the Alsops, Ben Bradlee—were friends of many years. But his associations went far beyond that to other men who were already senior correspondents when he, about the same age, was a junior congressman. It was quite natural for him, as President, to pick them up on Washington streets as they walked to work and talk to them about their work, their dates and their problems. This did some of them no journalistic harm. Rowland Evans went from *Herald Tribune* correspondent to syndicated columnist (with Robert Novak). Another, even closer friend, Charles Bartlett, went from correspondent for the *Chattanooga Times* to syndicated columnist.

Johnson had fewer personal friends among the press but typically they were more intense. Closest was William S. White, a fellow Texan, who, shortly after Johnson became President, wrote in his column: "For 30 years . . . I have intimately known Lyndon Johnson as I have never known any other public—or private—man." Mrs. Johnson's press secretary was Elizabeth Carpenter, who, with her husband, Leslie, used to run a moderately successful stringer bureau, mostly for Texas papers. After Johnson became President, Les Carpenter blossomed into a syndicated political columnist (with a growth in clientele reputed to be equal to that lost by Bartlett during the same period). Drew Pearson turned out to be distantly related by marriage to the new President and wrote a column in the form of an open letter to "My dear grandson, Lyndon." The new President was known to like and admire Philip Potter, who was content to remain a correspondent for the *Baltimore Sun*.

Johnson as President carried on a bustling cultivation of another level of the press. Shortly after his swearing in he unexpectedly visited Walter Lippmann. He sent a plane to Dallas to bring Mr. and Mrs. James Reston to the LBJ ranch for Christmas. He crashed a party given by Marguerite Higgins of Long Island *Newsday*. At parties he made sure to dance with wives of newspaper people.

At the managerial level the new President conducted an astounding series of lengthy luncheons and stag swimming pool splashes (which, unlike the Kennedy dunkings, were often without swim suits). He gave impromptu tours of his family quarters in the White House, including one of Mrs. Johnson's suite while she was bedridden with flu. (He comes honestly by this American home-showing impulse. He did it while majority leader, and at the grander Perle Mesta estate he bought when he was Vice-President, and with 1600 Pennsylvania Avenue; when Richard Nixon was Vice-President he also showed guests his closets.) He spent hours with executives of, among others, AP, UPI, *Time, Life, Newsweek,* the *Saturday Evening Post,* the *Wall Street Journal,* the *New York Herald Tribune,* the *Times,* ABC, NBC and CBS. He told most of them he read more than a dozen papers. He dropped in for lunch at the Forty-third Street mother church of the *New York Times* (on the same day that, back at the Hotel Carlyle, he expressed himself on the rival *Trib* in an idiom Harry Truman might have envied). He personally telephoned at length to reporters whose stories he liked (Cecil Holland, of the *Washington Star,* to take one). And his staff, implying that the boss was sitting beside them, complained bitterly to reporters whose stories were not liked. Douglas Kiker, of the *Herald Tribune,* for example, on the morning his story appeared saying the President was not doing so well on foreign affairs, got a White House telephone call at his home before breakfast.

Both the Kennedy and Johnson administrations involved themselves with the people of the press to a degree unprecedented in history. But there were important differences in the nature of the two relationships. The Kennedy entente was not always cordial, personally or managerially; there were jabs from the press and arrogance by some Kennedy press people. But the typical White House complaint then was about facts, not motives, and the President himself, always respectful of good minds and contemptuous of fools, steered clear of appearing to have vendettas against personalities.

The Johnson staff did not always do well by their boss. Their disputes were often over personal motives, on the assumption that a reporter ought to be "loyal" or at least "for" rather than "against." Some of the staff conducted press exercises that can only be described as clumsy. The Bobby Baker case broke while Johnson was still Vice-President and shortly thereafter a couple of the staff circulated among correspondents saying that the Johnson-Baker friendship had been exaggerated. Everyone on Capitol Hill knew of this friendship and it was folly to peddle a phony story to men who knew better. When the President's insurance agent gave irritating testimony about gifts to his client there followed high-level leaks of official government information tending to discredit the insurance agent. These efforts were ham-handed and left the President looking worse than before. The basic error here was not in trying to put the best face on the news—every normal human being tries that—but in ignoring the element of professionalism among press people. Most press people work by standards of performance that go beyond friendship and favors, and all of them—including those with weak standards—resent it if there is not at least some assumption that this is so.

This is not to say that President Johnson was not effective in his dealing with the news, for he was more effective than most of the Washington press thought he was. What appeared to some correspondents as incredible corniness was, in the shrewdness of President Johnson, impressive. For example, the President acknowledged that shutting off the White House lights didn't save much money but he judged better than newspapermen the impact of the symbolism of the lights-out policy.

His torrents of talk and his easy slipping on and off the record were bound to get him into trouble sooner or later. Officials and reporters were startled at the detail with which he recounted high-level conversations, sometimes with word-for-word dialogue and on treasured occasions with personal imitations, at which he was very good. But when he wanted to he could make Cal Coolidge look like a blabbermouth.

John Kennedy left his mark on many Washington correspondents, among them men not easily given to sentiment. When the assassination caught many columnists with obsolete columns about to be printed, the syndicates asked for new ones; Joseph Alsop, ordinarily the most relentless man in town, replied that he was too depressed by the news to write about it. Kennedy was a contemporary of most correspondents and culturally he was closer to them than any President they had known. More than ever newspaper people found themselves active in the governing process, sometimes disapproving and exploited, but changed for being a conscious part of the President's

thinking. A special excitement went out of Washington when John
Kennedy died.

If Kennedy's mind burned with a bright blue flame, Lyndon Johnson's was a roaring fire. It was an imprudent man in the news trade
who did not expect an alternation of painful blistering and warm
comfort from the new President who looked at the press not as a
hobby but as a bewildering, irritating problem. Lyndon Johnson concluded his relations with the press in bitterness and rejection.

11   The Camp in the Congo; or, Why
It Is That What the President Reads
in the *Post* and the *Times* Spoils
Other People's Breakfast

#

One day early in the Kennedy administration, White House correspondents, indulging a weakness for narcissism, asked the President's press secretary, Pierre Salinger, how many newspapers his boss read every day. Salinger, who was recovering from a couple of countermands that arose from the President's reading, replied sheepishly: "Too many."

Mr. Kennedy's voracious reading habits became legendary, leading to the popular notion that a President reads in order to keep his finger on the public pulse. This supposition assumes that newspapers arouse a mass public opinion that forces government to alter its course, that particular columnists provide new insights for national leaders and that hard-digging reporters astonish bureaucratic chiefs with exposés of skulduggery and sloth. All of these things happen from time to time, but not often. The chief impact of serious newspapers on national policy is more private and even more dramatic. In Washington the press is the only medium for presenting the same information to all national leaders at about the same time.

In a culture that is always in danger of drowning in paper and in a city where the leading industry is words, any piece of paper that is noticeable above the flood becomes important, and words that are so noticeable that they are seen by the President become supremely important. There is no faster or surer way to get a message before the

President of the United States than by having it appear as news in the *New York Times* and in the *Washington Post,* the two morning papers most widely noted in the capital.

The newspaper message seen by the President is not important merely for its educative effect on him. Its major influence is to infect the entire machinery of policymaking with the consciousness that the President and those below him have a dependable body of common knowledge. The result is more than current-events togetherness. The serious newspaper in Washington is a universal intelligence system and, in the case of the *Times,* provides the soundest selection available, inside the government or not, of those public events that need to be considered.

The fact that it is a blatantly public medium—seen simultaneously by bureaucrats, members of Congress, foreign ambassadors and agents, lobbyists and the citizenry at large—thrusts these events into the open, often to the consternation of the principals. It ends the peaceful coexistence of the elite in private conference. Republican must lay down poker hand and start fighting Democrat, trucking lawyer has to stop buying drinks for teamster lobbyist and attack the union, the United States has to stop the chess game at Paris and move troops in Indochina. Once the spotlight is on, all the clients start demanding results. In short, the government is forced to make decisions and to announce them. This has always been one of the effects of a vigorous, irreverent press, but it is intensified when a President not only reads, but lets everyone know it.

Mr. Eisenhower had a reputation for being an indifferent reader, and during the Kennedy administration New Frontiersmen liked to point to the contrast offered by their man. But the Kennedy appetite for newsprint signified more than a difference in personality and intellectual habits. It produced a special tone in the whole musculature of government decision, for it involved the President, in fact or in spirit, in policymaking far below the White House level. By the ritual of intense reading of the same newspapers, the President and his subordinates not only knew the same public things, but the subordinates knew the President knew.

Take, for example, one isolated story. On August 25, 1962, there appeared in the *New York Times* a dispatch from *Times* correspondent Lloyd Garrison, out of Thysville, the Congo, describing his visit to a small military training camp. It was a good firsthand account of a semisecret base operated inside the Congo by rebels from nearby Portuguese Angola, in preparation for future revolt against the Portuguese authorities. Long before Garrison's article appeared, this camp was well known to all concerned.

The Portuguese in Angola and in Lisbon wanted the camp shut down. They laid its continued existence to the United States, which supported the United Nations, which supported the central Congolese government, which permitted the camp to remain.

The American military knew about the camp and wanted it shut down because it further irritated the Portuguese, with whom the Department of Defense was negotiating for renewal of air base leases.

The Congolese, of course, knew about the camp and publicly approved of it, ostensibly as a gesture against colonialism, but more pragmatically as a bargaining weapon in their fight to establish dominance over the secessionist province of Katanga. Katanga, powerful and rich because of its production of ores through the Belgian-controlled Union Minière, shipped to the outside commercial world by way of a Portuguese railroad. The central government of the Congo saw the anti-Portuguese camp of the Angolans as a pawn in a future deal with the Portuguese: You close your railroad to Katanga and we'll close the camp.

The American State Department was divided. The powerful European Affairs section was against the camp since it further estranged Portugal and other allies during the Berlin crisis. The African Affairs section wanted a hands-off attitude because the camp offered possibilities of maneuver in settling the Katanga secession, because it would prevent the country's having to make another public choice between a European colonial ally and an African independence movement, and because the camp was operated by the more pro-Western faction of two Angolan rebel groups.

The highly active Union Minière lobby in New York was, of course, against the camp, as were most of the Belgian, French and British interests.

Despite all these concerns, the tiny camp in the Congo was still a small item in the daily decisions of the United States government. It was only a pebble in the daily avalanche of intelligence that pours into the State Department and has to be sifted, filed and passed upstairs. In continuing privacy all the conflicting forces pushed and shoved to get their way, in the hope that the struggle and the final decision would remain quiet. Nonpublicity would make it easier for the loser to take his consolation prize and go home.

Yet, no matter what his own bureaucracy decides to tell him, the policymaker has an outside source. Before the Secretary of State ever sees the pile of official documents on his desk, something else happens. At home he wakes up and reads the *New York Times* and the *Washington Post.*

By 7 A.M. on August 25, the other urgent-message member of the cabinet, Secretary of Defense Robert S. McNamara, was already in his chauffeur-driven car on the way to the Pentagon, reading the *Times* and the *Post.* Both secretaries did this while conscious of a third reader: at the same moment the President was doing precisely the same thing. In fact, the President was one up. The secretaries got the out-of-town Early City Edition of the *Times,* as did the President in bed. But at 8 A.M. a White House car would have returned from Union Station with a copy of the Late City Edition of the *Times.*

On the morning of August 25, it seems safe to assume, yet another breakfast was spoiled for Dean Rusk when he read Garrison's story. It took no angel from heaven to tell the secretary that from the White House, Congress, half a dozen embassies and a couple of undersecretaries, all hell would be breaking loose in a couple of hours. When he got to his office, the first thing the Secretary of State did was point to the *Times* story, telling his staff to get him everything they had on the situation, call a meeting that morning and get the camp closed.

The camp presumably still operated after the morning meeting. But for the first time men had to put their cards on the table and with everything before him the Secretary had to make a decision. What the newspaper story does, especially on foreign affairs, is to take the initiative away from the specialists and force a decision by politicians, or at least by men who must take politics into account. This is almost always a cruder compromise than if a decision were made in total secrecy. A news story in a serious and reliable paper can force decisions, sometimes in haste, often with attention out of proportion to importance, and at times under the worst possible circumstances. But such papers are the unannounced inspectors general of policymaking in government: they provide a consensus in an era of strong impulses to rule by insulated elites.

At times a foreign correspondent may bring genuinely new information into the government. In March 1962 a *New York Times* dispatch from Portuguese Guinea described a bitter protest against Portuguese authorities and official retaliation in that tiny colony. No American representative was there at the time, and confirmation of the report was almost impossible because of Portuguese secrecy. The government ordered research. It took a month to determine that the *Times* story had been essentially correct.

And there have been other cases. Dana Adams Schmidt's series of articles in the *Times* on Kurdistan caused high-level ripples in government. It is no secret that early in the war the newspaper's decision to send Homer Bigart to South Vietnam had a major influence on American activities there. Bigart and the better wire service correspondents in effect got firsthand information to the President, short-circuiting Vietnamese bureaucracy and the cumbersome and sometimes predisposed channels of American diplomatic and military reporting.

The *Washington Post* had been less authoritative on firsthand reporting from abroad, but it was read because it had a number of political columnists (Lippmann, Alsop, Childs, Pearson) and it was a carrier of much political news, including all the "unofficial official" news, or leaks. If Britain was holding back on a behind-the-scenes negotation on the Congo, an unattributed story on Britain's foot-dragging, presumably leaked from the White House, appeared in the *Post* and pushed the British.

On fast-breaking news, the Associated Press and United Press International can beat almost every method available to the government, short of the hotline. AP and UPI teleprinters operate in the White House and in the Pentagon (where the Secretary of Defense may see thirty or so takes in a typical day), and AP, UPI and Reuters have tickers in the Secretary of State's quarters. Tickers also operate behind the chambers of Congress.

The need for accuracy is obvious. On August 3, 1961, wire services (using suppositions shared by the police) inaccurately reported that two Cubans were in the process of hijacking an American jet airliner in Texas. Members of Congress kept running back to the tickers all afternoon and some worked themselves into such fury that they proposed resolutions declaring war on Cuba. The hijackers turned out to be a pair of Americans from Arizona.

For reporting of less visible events, the wire services do not come close to the experienced foreign correspondents of individual newspapers, some of whom are held in extraordinarily high regard by policymakers in government. There are officials who say they find such reporters more useful than foreign service, military and intelligence cables, partly because the correspondents are free from the bureaucratic stigma in making contacts, partly because they are able to concentrate on one target at a time, and—no small matter—they are generally briefer and easier to read.

The *Times* and *Post* correspondents in the field and their editor decide what every policymaker in the city of Washington will read sometime between six-thirty and nine-thirty every morning, and to that extent they condition the approach of leaders to every new day in the history of the republic. This is an awesome responsibility but, like the brain surgeon, the newspaperman is probably better off if he stays too busy to be awed.

When the President Unspeaks

In 1916, when he was safely out of the presidency, Theodore Roosevelt said: "one of our defects as a nation is a tendency to use what have been called weasel words." But earlier, when he was Vice-President (in fact, only four days before President McKinley was shot), TR nationalized the far more prudent adage: "Speak softly and carry a big stick."

One of the ways a prudent President can speak softly—or use weasel words, as some of our verbal Rough Riders would put it—is to pretend that he hasn't spoken at all. The most common method of doing this in Washington is to conduct a news conference under the Lindley Rules, named for Ernest K. Lindley, a former correspondent who later worked the other side of the street as a special assistant to the Secretary of State. Under the Lindley Rules, a creation of Franklin D. Roosevelt's press conferences, no meeting took place so far as the public is concerned. If reporters want to use something the nonspeaker has not said at the unmeeting, they must paraphrase the nonspeaker and attribute his ideas to their own intuition or some nameless source. This type of conference has come to be known as the "backgrounder."

The method is not limited to Washington. It is used in most capitals where press and public are kibitzers of government. Outside of government, it is employed by labor-management negotiators, by corporation executives and by university officials trying to fire the football coach. The ostensible purpose of letting an official speak to the press without being identified is to give the press the benefit of frank talk. If a high official speaks *ex cathedra* he is irretrievably stuck with whatever he says—so what he says on the record is likely to be cautious and conventional, especially if he is engaged in confidential negotiations on that particular subject.

Yet the official may want to say sharp things within earshot of the public, or to test a new idea before labeling it "Policy." Or he may want to say different things to different people. The Lindley Rules provide an escape from the source; an official may disavow his private statement if it jeopardizes an important objective.

This is either slightly two-faced or downright dishonest, depending on the latitude the official gives himself. It is pointless to pretend that politics and international relations are conducted with the naked honesty of the confessional. But it is wrong to assume that there are no limits whatever to the division between private talk and public policy. Too wide a gap destroys both private and public credibility of the man and his policies.

All of Washington uses and abuses the Lindley Rules. In March 1963, for example, Congress became self-righteously angry at the executive branch for using unattributed interviews to take cracks at legislative committees looking into the TFX matter, while the White House maintained a public appearance of neutrality. A four-fingered idiot would be able to count on one hand all the senators and representatives who have never taken advantage of being able to say one thing in private and another in public.

The most celebrated unattributed interview of that period was a background briefing held in the living room of the Palm Beach, Florida, vacation quarters of President Kennedy on December 31, 1962. For more than two hours the President answered questions from thirty-five White House correspondents, ranging over foreign and domestic issues as they looked at year's end. The session achieved fame for a number of reasons. For one thing, within six days the rule of nonattribution had been broken. For another, the resulting stories created irritation in Europe, or at least in European newspapers, this irritation being based on an inaccurate interpretation of what the President had said. It also stirred up some American editors to cast a pox on the whole institution of the backgrounder, apparently because they saw it merely as a public relations device or a cowardly act of refusing to take personal responsibility for what one says. Some of the proprietors of newspapers were further aggrieved because much of what the President told the word men privately on December 31 he had already said publicly for the hated medium of television on December 17.

In retrospect, the most startling side of this background conference was the way it demonstrated how the system of mass journalism multiplies error. It is now known precisely what the President said at Palm Beach, and it is known what ended up in foreign headlines (and domestic ones). They are not the same. The errors were printed not by the scandalmongers but by solemn and prestigious newspapers.

The agreement not to identify the President was broken by men who were not present and so not bound formally by the agreement. Only one of three hundred foreign reporters in this country was at Palm Beach (Alistair Cooke of the *Manchester Guardian*, now an American citizen). But the event was hardly secret.

When the story hit the Washington offices of the foreign correspondents it was hot news; it would become incandescent if they could only break through the transparent fiction of "the highest authority," which the men in Palm Beach had agreed to use as a substitute for "the President." Being under no agreement personally, they broke through rapidly. Louis Heren of the *Times* of London, after three days, had a quotation set in small type in a story, making plain it contained the words of President Kennedy. The next day Henry Brandon of the *Sunday Times* (no relation) had whole chunks quoted directly.

Brandon said he had been given permission by the White House. The White House says Brandon asked McGeorge Bundy, the President's special assistant, if he could quote directly and Bundy said it would be all right with him if Brandon would clear it with Pierre Salinger, the President's press secretary, or Robert Manning, assistant secretary of state for public affairs. Salinger and Manning say that they did not hear from Brandon.

A different case was that of C. L. Sulzberger. Tom Wicker was at the briefing for the *New York Times*, having agreed not to disclose that the source was the President. Sulzberger, also of the *Times* but in Paris, wrote a column on January 9 identifying the source. Earlier, as he had the year before, the *Times*'s Arthur Krock had implied in print that it was the President.

Like all etiquette, the Lindley Rules were violated when it became important for someone to break them. This violation seemed important to some foreign correspondents because they believed that the President had said something drastic about future relations in the Atlantic Alliance; if, in fact, he had said what the extreme stories had him saying, it would have become of commanding importance to know that it was, indeed, the President who had said these things.

What the President said was in answer to the following question:

Mr. President, this may be over-generalizing or over-simplifying, but a few things in recent months, like Cuba, the job at Nassau, the mention of the Congo, have given me the impression that you are moving in asserting a more positive leadership for the United States in this Alliance and in the world, having in mind what you said in the television interviews about how we have been financing the things all along.

The President replied:

Well, I think we are more aware, probably, that we are going to incur at intervals people's displeasure. This is sort of a revolving cycle. At least I think the United States ought to be more aware of it, and I think too often in the past we have defined our leadership as an attempt to be rather well regarded in all these countries. The fact is, you can't possibly carry out any policy without causing major frictions.

The President gave examples of places where complete agreement with the policy of one friend would displease other friends, as in the cases of France, India-Pakistan and the Congo. He concluded his answer:

So I think what we have to do is to be ready to accept a good deal more expressions of newspaper and governmental opposition to the United States in order to get something done than we have perhaps been willing to do in the past. I don't expect that the United States will be more beloved, but I would hope that we could get more done.

This was approximately four minutes of an hour-long discussion on foreign affairs. There was a ten-minute break for coffee, and then more than an hour on domestic affairs. The foreign affairs stories were to be held for use in morning papers of January 2, the domestic stories for afternoon papers of that day. The meeting broke up in the early afternoon. Before 6 P.M., a stenographer's verbatim transcript was posted. This made meaningless the later criticism of some British correspondents that the problem arose from the alleged inability of American correspondents to take shorthand. The first wire service story carried a transmission time of nine-thirty-three that night. There had been plenty of time to check the President's actual words.

The Associated Press lead was this:

President Kennedy intends to follow up his Cuban success by exerting stronger leadership over the West's Cold War policies—even at the risk of offending sensitive allies.

The United Press International lead said:

President Kennedy feels the Cuban missile crisis taught Russia a lesson and may have improved slightly the chances for keeping the world at peace in 1963.

The *New York Times* service lead said:

President Kennedy believes the onrush of Communist influence in the world was checked in 1962 and that the outlook for peace is slightly better in 1963.

One needs to read the entire transcript—or better still to have been at Palm Beach—to judge which of the President's dissertations made the best lead. The AP, at least to this reader, is not literally wrong in its wording, but does not accurately express the emphasis and tone of the President's statement. There is an important difference between resignation to inescapable fact and an aggressive statement that you will take the initiative regardless of others' feelings.

The AP lead was a sharpened paraphrase of what the President had said. And this more pointed paraphrase, implying a priority in the President's thinking, had news-making consequences of its own.

The sharpening process is encouraged by the intense competition among the news services, especially AP and UPI, which keep score on how many customers pick one wire service story over its rival's. The reporters are then told the score. All of this puts an extra premium on the punchy lead, the active verb, the vivid adjective.

These are not necessarily bad pressures—it is good to be as dramatic and specific as the facts allow—but they are dangerous in diplomacy and politics, as opposed to earthquakes and personalities.

Whatever the wisdom of the leads, or their accuracy, the AP story was about to dominate the field. The French and the German news agencies, and Reuters, used AP. Heren of the London *Times* was in Washington, where he received the UPI story and was about to fashion from it his version of how the President felt about foreign relations. But before he did, a neighbor on the ninth floor in the National Press Building, from the British Broadcasting Corporation, walked in and showed Heren the lead that had come off the BBC's AP ticker. Heren at once selected the AP version as his text for the day. (By this time the New York office of the London *Times* also had the AP version in hand and was urging it upon Heren.) On January 2 the *Times* carried this headline:

TOUGH LEADERSHIP RESOLUTION
BY PRESIDENT KENNEDY

Heren's story read, in part:

President Kennedy . . . is determined to provide strong leadership for the West, and strive harder to solve some cold war problems even if it hurts his closest allies.

He is willing to ignore allied criticism, which apparently is accepted as the price for progress. The action in Cuba, the scuttling of the Skybolt programme, and the dispatch of a military mission to the Congo, which were all undertaken without prior consultation, are apparently indications of the new tough policy towards the alliance.

Toughness has a certain appeal, even to the most sophisticated Americans . . . the tone is unmistakable . . . the President has made known that he will pace the foreign stage like a young lion. . . .

The next day in Paris, *Le Monde* carried the headline:

PRESIDENT KENNEDY HAS DECIDED TO DIRECT
THE WESTERN ALLIANCE WITHOUT WORRYING
ABOUT OBJECTIONS OF THE ALLIES

In a boldface preface, *Le Monde* said of the President's dissertation at Palm Beach: "The heart of the matter can be summed up in several words: It is indeed decided to go ahead and put back some order in the Atlantic Alliance, no matter what criticism and resistance may be encountered in Europe."

By January 6 the *Observer Weekend Review* in London was running a four-column spread under the head:

AULD ACQUAINTANCE FORGOT?

Underneath was a picture on the left of Winston Churchill with a quotation from his Fulton, Missouri, speech in 1946 on "the fraternal association of the English-speaking peoples." On the right was a picture of President Kennedy, captioned "The President's New Year Resolution at Palm Beach, 1963," and quoting what had been essentially the AP lead: "He is determined to provide stronger leadership for the West and strive harder to solve some Cold War problems even at the risk of hurting some of his closest allies."

Underneath this spreading chestnut there were some itemized "beach thoughts" such as: "The President feels that since America so predominantly pays the piper in general Cold War effort she should also call the tune."

At each step, as can be seen, more was written into what was reportedly said in the room at Palm Beach. What became obscured in the process, more easily in continental reporting than in American, was the distinction between what a man actually said and what the writer thought he meant. Both elements are necessary, especially where a man's words do not tell the whole story, or are meaningless without background. Both are needed, just as both vinegar and oil are needed in a good salad, but it is a poor mixer of salads who cannot tell oil from vinegar.

The Palm Beach briefing was a classic illustration of the fact that the news source has one picture in his head as he speaks, the reporter has another as he listens, the editor another as he decides how to play the story, and the consumer still another as he reads.

This difference in the points of view is one reason newsmakers are so often appalled at how their words are treated in print. The President shapes his words carefully to run the gauntlet of reporters-editors-Congress-foreigners-lobbies. But these words are then selected and paraphrased by a reporter whose words have to run the different gauntlet of personal perception–editor's judgment–reader interest.

This is good and proper, since a news source is seldom an objective judge of his own activities or words. If the press has any social function other than to operate typewriters it is to bring a set of values to news that is different from those of either the source or the reader.

But an intelligent news source has a reason for expressing things the way he does, and the better a reporter understands these reasons, the less violence he will do to the intent of the speaker. This is an argument for the specialist reporter. In the first half of the Palm Beach backgrounder perhaps State Department correspondents would have been better reporters than the White House regulars. Some White House regulars have competence in foreign affairs; many have not.

This case is also argument for keeping at a minimum the re-processings a reporter's story gets after he turns it in. There is an unavoidable loss in accuracy even with the best reporter—he simply can't reproduce the total scene, especially when he operates under such restrictions as the Lindley Rules. Thereafter the losses multiply. It is almost a mathematical rule that the larger the number of inter-mediaries between news event and print, the greater the distortion. There is also a geographical rule: the nearer to the scene the final version is written, the more the story will focus on the news event; the farther away, the more it will have its eye on the customers.

There is a great increase in this distortion when the news crosses to a foreign arena, since it must be fed to an audience with so different a set of news values that the strictly domestic reporter can hardly predict what picture his words will create in the minds of the distant alien.

Under the best of conditions, brute space makes a difference. The wire men, more than their colleagues, have to compress and sharpen. This is a severe pressure on a man handling a long, delicate story. The President and the reporters at Palm Beach spoke about eight thousand words about foreign affairs. The AP story on the "A" wire ran about fifteen hundred words; the *New York Times* story, about two thousand. The AP's shift in focus came not from the usual lack of time and need for space, but perhaps from the lifetime habit of operating under such conditions. The *Times* story kept carefully close to the President's own words; the AP, in not much less space, sharp-ened and paraphrased.

The incident cast a momentary pall on the presidential back-grounder as an institution. The first reaction of the White House was "never again." But this really means: "Well, hardly ever." The back-grounder is too useful—to both sides—to abandon. The President needs to mass-produce some education of the press to his problems. Merely as a method of maintaining cordial professional relations, the backgrounder has its own self-serving function. For the press, any time the President of the United States wants to sit down and talk, it is mandatory for professional reasons to listen carefully.

One must report one shocking statement by the President at Palm Beach that went unreported. In one portion John Kennedy, no doubt still under the strain of Cuba, Nassau and de Gaulle, succumbed to Winston's Syndrome: he used "like" when he should have used "as." But in the next sentence he returned to the English language, as a President should.

(As this book went to press, the *Washington Post* announced that it would no longer take part in group background sessions in which rules forbid informing readers the source of information.)

13   LBJ and the Press; or, The Commander-in-Chief Thought He Was Editor-in-Chief

\#

In the first year of his presidency, Lyndon Johnson courted the press with manic zeal. He had coveys of publishers in for lunch and naked dives into the White House swimming pool; he invited children of reporters to a special press conference; he danced indefatigably with wives of correspondents at state banquets; and he held a succession of quick news conferences in his office, ranch, airplane and on his lawn, confessing to the reporters what was on his mind, soul and viscera. If the press was ideologically opposed to the Democratic party, Lyndon Johnson refused to accept its hostility, and instead of sparring with the papers in the ring of public opinion, he fell into a clinch from which newspapermen found it hard to stand back and swing haymakers.

But the heavyweight champion finally ended this waltz, stepped back and poked the press in the chops. One year and six days after he entered the White House, Lyndon Johnson ended his honeymoon with the press and began acting like a normal President of the United States: he criticized reporters, he hinted that they had endangered the national welfare and he politely told them to go to hell. Some of his indictment was ungenerous, but it was inevitable and healthy. It was healthy in the manner of an elderly woman we know of who was administered an opiate in preparation for minor surgery and in her unrestrained state delivered some long-standing grudges she harbored against her friend the surgeon. The rattled physician gestured to have the patient put under deeper anesthesia but before she went under, the lady announced: "Open expression of hostility is good mental health." And so it is.

The President's exasperation with the press was inevitable and healthy in another way. The public official and the press have different roles in a democracy, something the official almost always forgets and the press sometimes does. The press is not an instrument of official policy and reporters will sometimes outrage a President. The papers will talk of impending appointments or of diplomatic negotiations when open talk creates maddening problems for the President. They will speculate about policies when the policymakers themselves have not yet decided what to do. They will listen patiently to officials who put one construction on events and then rush into print with a different construction. In addition to such unrestrained behavior, the press is often uncomprehending, sometimes wrong and occasionally malicious.

President Johnson's reversion to historic form was nonetheless ungenerous, because he had enjoyed a spectacularly good press. This was not because American newspapers have an uncontrollable passion for Democrats, as Senator Goldwater implied, but because the President and the press had just completed a strange and unique year which could not serve as a model for anything in the future.

The unusual year began with the assassination of John F. Kennedy. In the aftermath of the tragedy the press did not treat the new President with its normal irreverence. It is embarrassing to go back and look at news stories, features and syndicated columns of the post-assassination period, with their lavish praise of Lyndon Johnson and their extravagant assurance to the country of his wise leadership. The country at that moment was wounded and the press was disinclined to pick fights with the new President in a time of trial.

The press was also experiencing a genuine revelation in the unfolding qualities of a Lyndon Johnson they had not suspected. Some of the gushiness of the time undoubtedly arose from reporters who expected the worst and discovered something good.

Not long afterward came the 1964 election campaign and this, too, created a special journalistic condition. During campaigns of recent years the press has taken an unnatural stance, restraining its usual

instinct to leap through each chink in every man's armor, for fear
that it may appear to be unfair during an election campaign. Ironically, Senator Goldwater intensified this withdrawal by making the
press more self-conscious than ever.

During both these periods—the recovery from the trauma of the
assassination and the campaign—Lyndon Johnson used the press
without shame or restraint. "Used the press" is not written here with
a sneer. A President would have to be an idiot not to use the press.
Every intelligent politician uses the press or, to use an ancient term,
manages the news. If the press does not begin with this assumption
then it ought to go into a less demanding business, like buying
wooden nutmegs. The press has to cull the output of every news
source for false or exclusively self-serving propaganda. But during
the post-assassination and election periods, its guard was down.

So in early 1965 the President came upon normal journalistic times
and he, like every President before him, didn't like it. More than
most Presidents, he cried out when he was hurt in print. It is instructive to see just what he complained of in his conference in Johnson
City on November 28, 1964, when he read the press a lesson. In the
past Mr. Johnson had, in the words of Paul Healy of the *New York
Daily News,* "tried killing the press with what he regarded as kind-
ness." On November 28 a few excessively sensitive reporters thought
he was just trying to kill them.

In his opening sentence, the President said that in discussing the
Atlantic Alliance, the press and broadcast commentators had shown
a "neglect of first principles." Presumably he referred to widespread
comment that NATO was in "disarray." The President said that the
basic fact was that there is no question of this country's commit-
ment to Europe and that "there are no problems which we cannot
solve together." The President obviously felt that the press was
accentuating the negative and, in highlighting the allies' differences,
was overshadowing their ultimate unity.

Yet the Alliance had been in trouble. Some of the President's
advisers had been saying openly that something serious was wrong.
Visible events abroad were evidence that de Gaulle was on a collision
course on a number of issues. The multination force had a shaky
future. The President couldn't talk about these things, or act on
them, during the campaign for fear foreign policy would get torn apart

in electioneering. The press, too, was muted, concerned with the campaign. The election over, foreign policy tumbled into the headlines again.

Should correspondents respond to the President by writing how strong the Alliance was? Almost by natural law the press is the dye that lodges in diseased cells of the national tissue. The PR men are the ones who accentuate the positive. It is understandable that the President has to quiet down allies who are getting jumpy and it is forgivable if he occasionally blames the press. But it can get to be a bad habit. What is surprising is how many sins the press gets away with because people blame it for the wrong things.

The President also had unkind things to say about the press's treatment of the subject of Vietnam. "When you crawl out on a limb," he told the reporters, "you always have to find another one to crawl back on." The President poked fun at the newspaper stories about recommendations within the government to increase the military involvement in Vietnam, hinting that they were invented out of thin air: "I don't know whether you have a black sheet that you take out and rewrite every time we have a meeting on Vietnam. . . ." He said he would meet his ambassador to South Vietnam, Maxwell Taylor, that very week and anticipated "no dramatic announcement to come out of these meetings except in the form of your speculation."

But in Vietnam the United States government found itself out on a limb, trying desperately to crawl back. As a matter of fact, when the President and Secretary of Defense Robert McNamara did meet with Maxwell Taylor, they came out of their conference with McNamara saying—unaware that reporters could hear him—"It would be impossible for Max to talk to these people without leaving the impression the situation is going to hell." It would be a strange press that did not report this remark and speculate on its meaning. Shortly thereafter, the situation did go to hell. Was the press wrong, or simply embarrassing the policymakers?

At the same news conference on the Pedernales, the President was asked whether J. Edgar Hoover was correct when he told some woman reporters that the President had said Hoover could remain chief of the FBI as long as Johnson was President. The President referred them to his press secretary, George Reedy. When Reedy was

asked whether or not the President had said that to Hoover, his reply
was: "I'm not going into that question."

The lessons of the First Normal Press Conference are several:

Irritation, conflict and gamesmanship are inevitable in the relations of President and press. The President cannot be candid all the
time on all subjects, but just because the President won't speak does
not mean the press—or anyone else—cannot think. Furthermore, the
President will often use the press for his own and the national purpose, and if, as so many people say with justice, the President needs
a thicker skin when it comes to criticism from the press, the press
needs a tough hide, too.

The press is delighted to accept a high-level leak from an official
who, perhaps with White House acquiescence, is trying out a new
policy with public opinion. If the policy runs into trouble and the
White House denies paternity, that is part of the deal. It is a common
and often useful charade, but there is a limit to how much it can be
used before it becomes a disservice to everyone.

These inevitable vexations increase as access to abundant reliable
information decreases. One trouble with Lyndon Johnson was that he
was his own press secretary and a very busy man. John Kennedy also
was his own press secretary. The last press secretary who really spoke
with authority was James Hagerty and one criticism of him was that
he was his own President. President Johnson used to make a number
of appeals to the White House regulars. One was: "Why don't you
fellows do what the *Baltimore Sun* does? Now the *Sun* always checks
out its stories." The *Sun* is an excellent paper and its senior Washington man, Philip Potter, is a first-rate reporter, but he had a rare relationship with the President that opened many doors and this could
not be shared by the 1,300 correspondents accredited to the White
House—or even by all the White House regulars.

Another favorite Johnson injunction was: "If you want to know
anything, just ask. Ask George Reedy, and if he doesn't know, ask
Jack Valenti. If Jack doesn't know, ask Bill Moyers. If Bill doesn't
know, then ask me." All of these men were busy, and while Reedy
was the man whose job it was to deal with the press, he didn't know
everything his boss was doing. Even prestigious reporters for powerful papers couldn't always get Valenti or Moyers the same day they
called. And not many correspondents were going to ask for an ap-

pointment with the President of the United States on every story they
got for which they could not get confirmation from Reedy, Valenti
or Moyers. Kennedy's staff men were more accessible to the press,
and there were more of them who had a clear idea of what was going
on. Johnson's informed policy men were fewer—and less inclined to
talk.

As President Johnson shaped his own administration, selecting his
own men and developing his own policies, the sources of authoritative
information dwindled. Appointments to office and new policies developed, like photographs, in the dark. One result was added depen-
dence on subterranean journalism in Washington. There was a hierarchy of devices for getting exclusive stories or background. In its
quintessence, it was represented by Walter Lippmann, whose home was
visited by an extraordinary succession of authorities from whom was
extracted the world's best information. Near the summit were men like
James Reston, who could talk to any official of the government they
chose, beginning with the President. Below that were the small informal groups of senior correspondents who on occasion gathered in
hotel banquet rooms to listen to an important personage speak without attribution. Forming the base were regular, organized groups
whose meetings were practically announced—postcards were sent to
members—and whose speakers were introduced by something like:
"Gentlemen, let me remind you that we meet under the Lindley
Rule: this meeting was never held and anything you wish to say must
be said on your own authority and not attributed to the speaker, or to
any official or department of the government."

The guest of honor on such occasions usually began with a witty,
discursive talk while the assembled correspondents waited for the
policy bomb the official wanted to drop, which explained why he
accepted (or provoked) the invitation in the first place. Both sides
used each other in this ritual.

In the absence of normal access to authoritative people around
President Johnson, and of some systematic, predictable access to the
President comparable to John Kennedy's announced press conferences, the extracting of lower-level information went on in groups and
individually. It was a game to find the source of a scoop by trying to
remember which official source was seen having lunch with which reporter at the Federal City Club, or the Metropolitan, or the National

Press. Presidents have been known to track down such combinations personally and let their man know that they did.

On another level, the President and his aides indulged in more important subterranean journalism. Here the White House jeopardized its influence with the press corps. The specific meaning and probable consequences of official policy statements, especially in foreign affairs, usually were left vague. The government may have wished to warn a foreign power, or hold out hope, or bluff, or experiment, or signal a change in its policy. But it did not want to show its total hand before it saw the foreign reaction, hoping to get an optimum response. The press could report only these public generalities but the serious reader wanted to know what they meant. The correspondent usually didn't know precisely what they meant but the government official did. So the correspondent went to or was called in by the official, who told him, without attribution.

A scenario for such an episode, based on an actual case, goes like this:

The President makes a speech. He includes a vaguely worded sentence about Vietnam. The wire service and other important correspondents lead with more explicit statements on other subjects. A White House aide close to the President (Valenti) tells correspondents that they picked the wrong lead, that the Vietnam sentence reflects a grave behind-the-scenes policy decision to get really tough in Asia if the Communists continue their intervention in Southeast Asia. The leads are changed accordingly.

All Presidents exploit such private guidance and most of them occasionally find it expedient to repudiate it publicly, sometimes for high policy reasons but often to avoid personal embarrassment and to shift blame to the press. Kennedy used words precisely and employed his private guidance—and its public repudiation—with an eye for future credibility both with newsmen and foreign leaders (who are quite aware of the official guidance). Johnson was less precise in his use of words but, more important in this respect, he too often used his private access to correspondents for short-term objectives. In letting loose a shotgun criticism of his White House press corps, lumping together their own deductions with those they used from his own people as wrong and irresponsible, the President became the ultimate loser. The danger to him was not mere pique among newsmen, though there was some of that, but that the press—out of nervousness at being dupes and official propagandists, aggravated by the threat of public ridicule by the President partly for what they did on his behalf—could become immune to any official guidance whatever. This would have been a loss to newsmen, who need to know what is behind the blandness of public utterances, but it would also have been a loss to government, which would have needlessly thrown away its capital of credibility.

For those who think that Washington reporting ought to stick to objective fact alone, consider what happened when this was applied to so simple an exercise as police reporting.

J. Edgar Hoover was considered the most unimpeachable source there was on crime, but in an interview with eighteen women reporters, practically all of it on the record, error was not lacking. In pressing his claim that too lenient courts had encouraged crime in the streets, Mr. Hoover said Barry Bingham had been robbed recently across the street from the Sheraton Park Hotel in Washington, when in fact it was not the Binghams, but Mr. and Mrs. Mark Ethridge, and it had not been recently but several years before. Mr. Hoover has also said that it was unsafe to walk in New York's Central Park in broad daylight, to which another authority on crime, the New York Police Commissioner, replied: "It's the kind of statement that people make all the time without any basis in fact."

True candor at high levels of government is not ordinarily displayed on the record but it is not impossible. It might be rewarding to try it sometime. On April 4, 1935, reporters asked Harry Hopkins, Franklin Roosevelt's relief administrator, about criticism by New Yorkers of a new Roosevelt program, and Hopkins replied—for the record: "Dumb people criticize something they do not understand, and that is what is going on up there—God damn it! . . . I have no apologies to make."

There is even something to be said for a simple refusal to answer. Ernie Pyle once wrote about Hopkins: "It tickled me the way you would say, 'I can't answer that,' in a tone that almost says out loud, 'Now you know damn well when you asked me that I couldn't answer that. . . .' "

Candor would be a noble experiment.

14   The President Just Another Flack?

#

I once had a student in aerial navigation whose calculations told him that we were going to reach Albuquerque, New Mexico, at a certain time. At that time we reached El Paso, Texas. "But that's impossible," the student said. He shook his log with all his computations in front of my face. "I've got the figures to *prove* we're in Albuquerque." He did, too. But we were in El Paso.

This episode came to mind when President Johnson in a 1965 press conference described the care with which he reached his decision to send the Marines to Santo Domingo. "I had 237 individual conversations during that period and about thirty-five meetings with various . . ."

The President was a lover of statistics and of appearances and in the fierce gamesmanship that developed in the White House he proved himself an indefatigible practitioner of the art of public relations. This presented special problems for the press corps, but not simply because a President tried to put himself in the best light, because all do that.

Joseph Kraft, writing in *Harper's*, believed the President's troubles with the press "stem largely from the inability of the press to see the President as just another flack."

What does it mean if the press has to view the President of the United States as "just another flack"?

The problem is not the existence of public relations in the White House, which has to consider its "image" if for no other reason than to know whether it is being understood. But there is flackery and flackery, and the White House has pushed the techniques of PR to the point of negative returns.

Some White House deceptions are justified as part of the job. President Eisenhower would have been wiser to refuse comment on the U-2 shot down over Russia. As a national leader the President has to keep himself open to negotiations for the national good and if he publicly associates himself with all the dirty tricks that go on behind the scenes he damages his power—not because he tells the other side anything it doesn't privately know, but because he becomes a public symbol of the dirty tricks, with whom other national leaders cannot negotiate. Precisely because the President is more than a promoter of his own program and reputation, more than a proprietor of government agencies, but is also a symbol of national aims and values, it is important that he be listened to—and speak—as something more than a shrewd public relations man.

Some of the deceptions have been important. For weeks President Johnson told the public it was being misled by reporters who said the government was considering widening the war in Vietnam. The reporters were correct and the President wrong. The White House implied that it consulted the Organization of American States before committing troops to the Dominican Republic, but it never told the OAS beforehand that it was considering troops.

Other illusions are of interest chiefly within the trade, such as the time President Johnson gave a backgrounder in Texas but asked correspondents to put on a Washington dateline (which most did).

The problem was partly the astonishing portion of attention Lyndon Johnson gave to public relations. No President monitored his public image with more zeal. He often pulled popularity poll results out of his pocket. He added up hours of time given to the press and it was enormous, though much of it was ritualistic or non-useful. In one extended session a French correspondent whispered to an American that he had a Paris deadline coming up and had to leave. The President was holding forth on the White House south balcony. The American whispered back that the Frenchman couldn't possibly leave. "But we've been here for an hour and a half and he is saying nothing and I have a deadline." The American hissed: "Would you leave if Charles de Gaulle were doing this?" The Frenchman stiffened and whispered: "Charles de Gaulle would not spend fifteen minutes talking about the rust on his balcony."

The President and his staff seemed to ring like burglar alarms whenever and wherever the name "Johnson" appeared in print or was uttered on the air. A small item in a west Texas paper mentioned Billie Sol Estes in connection with the President in a three-paragraph story on the inside; the editor claims he got a telephone call from the White House in time to kill the item in later editions. One television correspondent was awakened in the middle of the night by the White House, which had heard that he planned to make some critical remarks the next day. A newspaper correspondent wrote a critical morning story and got three telephone calls from White House aides before breakfast. The *New York Review of Books*, a medium-highbrow publication, ran a scathing review of Johnson's Vietnam policy and its editors got a phone call from a White House aide suggesting that in the future they have Vietnam books reviewed by Joseph Alsop (who approved of the Johnson policy).

The President had three television sets for simultaneous viewing of the three major networks, plus an AP and UPI ticker. Apparently he watched them more closely than some of the editors. One night a startled wire service editor in Washington got a White House call later preserved in the house organ, *U.P.I. Reporter*, as follows:

"Hello?"

"Hello, Pat, this is Lyndon Johnson."

"Yes, Mr. President."

"Say, I have here . . . (pause) . . . A101N from Johnson City, Texas, about the homestead, by Kyle Thompson. Let's see . . . (pause) . . . you say in there that there's going to be a fee for the tour. Well, that's not right at all. The idea is to give it to the people."

"Just a minute, Mr. President, and I'll get the story."

"You see what it says. It says 'the home was opened to the public for fee tours.' That isn't right. You see, it's for free. That's the idea. Do you see that?"

"Yes, Mr. President. It looks like they dropped the 'r' in the word 'free.' I guess they omitted it in transmission."

"Well, Pat, it sure does mean just the opposite of what we mean."

"It sure does, Mr. President. I'll fix it."

"Well, we want it to be free."

"Certainly, Mr. President. I'll straighten it out right away."

"I'd appreciate it if you would clean this up for me."

"I certainly will, Mr. President."

"We hope you will take the necessary steps to straighten this out."

"Yes, sir, Mr. President."

"Thank you, Pat."

"Thank you for letting us know, Mr. President."

But the problem is not just quantity of presidential time and intervention. Some of it was less meticulous than his editing of UPI typos, and some had such implausible endings that his credibility was harmed. He liked to be the miracle worker, so he took petty pains to knock down stories predicting what he would do. In December 1964 he complained that the *Washington Evening Star* reported falsely that he would propose a 3 percent pay raise for federal workers.

At about the same time, the President accused the *Washington Post* of erroneously stating that he planned to ask for a $4 billion cut in excise taxes. "The President is described as feeling that the $4 billion figure couldn't be further wrong," the news story read. Press secretary George Reedy said: "That figure bears no relationship to any decision that has been made." The President proposed an excise tax cut of $3.964 billion, which bears a relationship to $4 billion as 99.1 to 100.

Nor was it unknown that a responsible White House aide would confirm a reporter's story before it was printed, and after the published story caused unexpected embarrassment, another equally responsible White House aide would tell reporters that the story was wrong and was never checked with the White House.

While doing all this, the President maintained sympathetic relations with editors and publishers beyond anything known before. Lyndon Johnson was the only Democratic President in this century who seemed to be on better terms with newspaper publishers than with the working press. This isn't bad; it is merely astonishing. I. F. Stone, an incorrigible heretic in a town with increasing pressures for journalistic orthodoxy, wrote: "Johnson sometimes seems to think the Constitution made him not only commander-in-chief of the nation's armed forces but editor-in-chief of its newspapers."

Among the institutional casualties of this crushing program of public relations were the press briefings by the press secretary, which were decreasing in content, and the presidential press conference, which became increasingly rhetorical. Even the semiconfidential backgrounder was often reduced to an absurdity. On April 7, 1965, for example, such a session was held to give prior interpretation of the President's Johns Hopkins University speech offering "unconditional" discussions on Vietnam. The briefing was given in the White House by Secretary of Defense Robert McNamara, Acting Secretary of State George Ball and special assistant McGeorge Bundy. Ordinarily it is not cricket to print names of briefing officers but in this case the White House disclosed them by staging a make-believe start of the briefing for television and radio for the 6 P.M. newscasts to help build public interest in the speech.

When it came to the nonattributable Q and A, the cameras were shut off, but the same spirit of charade continued to pervade the session. Max Frankel of the *New York Times* asked why the government had waited so long to make public its aims and its basis for settlement in Vietnam. Secretary Ball said that there was no delay, that the government had always had the position presented in the President's speech.

"Are you saying," Frankel asked, "that this speech is not news, that we should treat it as old stuff?" Ball replied that the government had always held the same position, though the "formulations" might be new and, he added as a parting shot, "it may be a little clearer to you." To which John Scali, ABC diplomatic correspondent, rose to say: "Since this has all been said before, would the Secretary please refresh the reporters' memories on the last time anyone in the government offered unconditional discussions on Vietnam?" There was general laughter and no answer.

The White House seemed so obsessed with keeping the news record favorable that it was defensive about firsthand journalism that it could find useful. The press helped dispel some of the wild confusion within government on the Dominican coup d'etat with reporting from the scene that was better than official diplomatic and military accounts.

The same was true in Vietnam. John Mecklin, chief information officer in Saigon during the time when David Halberstam of the *Times* and Malcolm Browne of the AP were official dirty words, wrote in his book, *Mission in Torment,* that Halberstam and Browne were essentially correct in their reporting and the government essentially wrong.

The White House obsession with PR would be easier to handle if it came from another source. Most correspondents learned to cope with flackdom a long time ago: they react when special pleaders originate news; they recognize the implausibly rosy release; they instinctively check with the opposition; they treat with contempt a man who deliberately flimflams them.

What is special here is Kraft's observation: most reporters had trouble looking at the President as just another flack. He was not just another flack. He was a PR man in his obsession with image, his unrestrained attempts to create illusion for tactical reasons and his concern with appearances no matter how implausible. But he was also President of the United States, carrying the burdens of his office seriously.

The problem was that Lyndon Johnson appealed to reporters with all the dignity and power of his position as President and when this did not produce the results he wanted, he began manipulating them and the news in ways that are not highly regarded even at the Press Club bar. He was trying to have it both ways. The President was too valuable a source in the competition for news to be ignored as a lesser PR man would be. But deeper than that was the conflict the President created in many serious correspondents who respected the office of President and the man in it, but whose professional standards told them that what was going on was common, ordinary press agentry.

The President and his aides often seemed to ignore the demands of professionalism upon correspondents, which require exercise of independent judgment based not on personality or pressure but on honest discrimination. Too often correspondents were asked to choose between disrespect for the reader and disrespect for the President.

One simple answer may be to report the unabashed intervention of the White House into the news process. The dialogue in *U.P.I. Reporter* was seen widely in the trade, but it was not on the UPI wire. Ordinarily this would be healthy avoidance of narcissism. But perhaps the time has come to report the President not only as originator of news but also as editor of it.

| 15 | The Great Nixon-Agnew Media Con Game; or, A Few Plain Facts About the Politics of Newspapers |

\#

Shortly after Richard Nixon and Spiro Agnew took office, some *Washington Post* reporters began avoiding conversations with people who sat next to them in airplanes. When they registered at hotels they stopped filling in the space marked "Organization." If someone came right out and asked them what they did for a living, at least one of them simply said, "I work in Washington," adopting a favorite euphemism of employees at the Central Intelligence Agency.

Of all the public relations victories of the Nixon administration, the greatest has been against the presumed experts in the field, the American newspaper establishment. The President's anointed agent in this, Vice-President Agnew, has succeeded in impressing a large part of the American public and of American publishers that the media of this country are biased toward liberalism, that this is contrary to the basic values of the country and, of course, of the Nixon administration.

The chief targets for this in printed journalism have been the *Washington Post* and the *New York Times*. A random selection of businessmen and affluent ladies flying in airliners is likely to make a trip unpleasant for a representative of the *Post* or *Times*, and where once a newspaper connection almost guaranteed a nice hotel room, since 1968 it may turn up a broom closet where the air-conditioner doesn't work.

In every part of the country there are militant folk who never before knew or understood the words but who now recite at slightest provocation the Agnewite rhetoric about "liberal bias," "monopoly media" and "separation of news and opinion," and enter into lengthy disquisitions on "objectivity," frequently interrupted while they turn on Paul Harvey or offer as exemplary models William Buckley and Ralph de Toledano.

It's not a bad thing that Washington correspondents get into arguments on airliners or have to sleep in an occasional hotbox. They've been getting preferential treatment for a long time because they're journalists and it is good for their egalitarian souls to learn how the other half of the privileged live.

The irony is that Agnew is right—the newspapers of this country are out of step with the electorate and it is ironic because they are massively out of step in the direction opposite the one that Nixon-Agnew claim.

The voters of the country, including those in "middle America," are basically Democratic and not Republican, and at least fifty-fifty liberal. The newspapers are overwhelmingly Republican and conservative.

Political parties command decreasing reflex obedience. But whether on a party or an ideological basis, the press is out of step and so is the rhetoric (but not necessarily the program implications) of the Nixon administration. Mr. Nixon, being shrewd, must know this. He plays a two-code game, signaling conservatives with his administration's attacks on the "liberal press" and other tribal drumbeats, and attracting liberal voters with trips to China and attempts to change welfare programs.

It is curious, then, that the chief consumer of this double press agentry has been the publishing fraternity, which has been wringing its hands denying the guilt attributed to it by Mr. Agnew. Publishers have been living in a political dream world for a long time, out of touch with economic and social realities, if one believes their editorials, and fearful of the socialism and liberalism and Democratic tendencies of their reporting staffs. If Mr. Nixon knows better, most newspapers don't seem to. The President and Vice-President have found the publishers' inner fears and they play on them with all the flamboyant virtuosity of Liberace at the piano.

There are about 1,750 daily papers in the country, of which the two most powerful in national policy are the *Post* and the *Times*. They are justifiably singled out for special attention. Their influence is disproportionate partly because they happen to be delivered to important people in the capital every morning. But that isn't the only reason. With all their faults, they are better than other papers in their selection of news, completeness of reporting and knowledge of national social and economic developments. They are more conservative on many issues than their readers; they only appear to be far out in comparison with their 1,748 siblings.

Mr. Agnew has talked about "strident opposition on the front page," has demanded that "a broader spectrum of national opinion should be represented," has condemned "editorialists in Washington and New York . . . their vilification and sarcastic invective . . . learned idiocy," and the "sheer hypocrisy . . . [of] the eastern media."

Later, Mr. Agnew had to extend "eastern" to a few papers in California, Arkansas, Missouri and Georgia, so that "eastern," like "middle America," is no longer geographical but ideological.

I guess Mr. Agnew has not been reading the average paper in Middle America. It is completely conservative and has no place for "a broader spectrum" of opinion. It is also out of step with its readers.

An important man in the Nixon administration likes to talk about "the real America west of the Appalachians." The same man, irritated by a group of Washington journalists, said bitterly: "You're all from New York, anyway." None of them happened to be from New York, but it was true that two of them were Jews, which in Wasp suburbia is often synonymous with "New York."

Official irritation with the press is inevitable. Stalin probably was irritated from time to time with *Pravda* and *Izvestia*. But political reality calls for some simple facts.

For as long as any living politician can remember the daily press has been overwhelmingly Republican, and it still is. Of dailies that endorsed a presidential candidate in the Nixon-Kennedy campaign of 1960, 84 percent endorsed Nixon. When Nixon ran against Humphrey in 1968, 80 percent endorsed Nixon. These were not just the small papers. Nixon had 83 percent of daily circulation for him in 1960 and 78 percent in 1968. And though Nixon people like to castigate the big-city press in contrast to the "real American" papers in the smaller cities, huge metropolises such as Los Angeles, Chicago, Detroit, Cleveland and Philadelphia had all their major papers for Nixon.

But maybe presidential endorsements don't typify a paper's display of ideas day in and day out. Might a conservative paper pick political columnists of the opposite persuasion? Two-thirds of papers that regularly endorse Republican candidates have a preponderance of conservative columnists.

Is it possible that Republican papers might endorse a Republican candidate and pick conservative columnists but are not conservative when it comes to specific issues? Representative Bob Eckhardt, a Texas Democrat, polled a sample of American dailies and found that two-thirds of the papers that endorsed Republican candidates also supported the conservative position on ABM, the Carswell Supreme Court nomination, the Cambodian invasion, the McGovern-Hatfield antiwar amendment and Agnew's statement against dissenters.

Congressman Eckhardt found some interesting regional variations. Northeastern papers—remember the "eastern media"?—were more conservative than the national average and more conservative than—remember "middle America"?—the Midwest.

The Eckhardt survey included the 125 papers in the country that have circulations over 100,000. Two-thirds of these papers answered.

But still, is it possible that newspapers might endorse Republicans, print conservative columnists, editorialize in favor of conservative issues, but still counterbalance this with pro-liberal bias in their news columns? In the mid-sixties I looked at the current published studies of political bias in the news. There were eighty-four systematic studies that found significant bias. There was a very high correlation between editorial policy and news bias. Of the eighty-four studies of bias, seventy-four found pro-Republican bias in the news in papers with pro-Republican editorial policies. There were seven instances of pro-Democratic bias in papers with pro-Democratic editorials. Only in three of the eighty-four cases was news bias the opposite of editorial position. So where political bias in the news is found, it is over-whelmingly pro-Republican and pro-conservative.

Could it be that where there is pro-Republican bias, perhaps it reflects the values of the readers and voters? The opposite is true.

It has been an article of faith among right-wing theologians that there is a conservative tide in the country, that fear of crime and opposition to racial equality has been successfully mobilized to turn the voters to the right on all issues.

The most sensitive measure of the country's practical political feeling is how the people in each of the 435 congressional districts vote for their member of the House of Representatives every two years. The votes of these congressmen are tabulated on the basis of conservative and liberal issues and published by *Congressional Quarterly*. (This is a better measure than party affiliation. The Democrats have a clear majority in the House and Senate but some Southern Democrats are more conservative than the most reactionary Republican and some Republicans more liberal than the average Democrat.) In the 1969–1970 session of Congress, the conservatives had a slight edge: 54 percent. But if there is a tide it seems to be going the other way. The 1970 elections shifted the majority to the liberals.

How do the politics of the press compare with the politics of the people at the grass roots—the "real Americans" out there in their home districts?

Using the more conservative Congress of 1969–1970, there were representatives from 222 districts that voted more than half the time with the congressional conservative coalition, an alliance of conservative Republicans and Democrats. If one counts a Nixon endorsement in 1968 as a sign of conservatism in a paper, then the major papers with significant circulation in each of these 222 conservative districts gave their congressman strong support. These 222 conservative districts had 430 conservative papers and 88 liberal ones (counting, for these purposes, endorsement of Humphrey in 1968 as liberal).

In the same period there were 202 liberal districts. These had 360 conservative papers in them and 115 liberal papers. So the conservatives in their districts had a five-to-one advantage in newspaper support.

In liberal districts, the liberal congressmen and their voters had three-to-one opposition from the daily papers. The absence of liberal papers among liberal Americans is one of the astonishing facts of media life. There were seventy-nine congressional districts in 1968 that showed every available sign of overwhelming desire by the voters for liberal Democracy: a majority voted against Nixon and Wallace, and a majority voted for a liberal congressman who delivered liberal votes in Washington. But these seventy-nine districts had no liberal or pro-Democratic papers at all, and 130 pro-Republican ones. There were only five districts that both voted for Nixon or Wallace and elected a conservative congressman that were served solely by a pro-Humphrey paper.

There is much talk of a "liberal conspiracy" in the press but the real question is how liberal electoral politics survives at all with the overwhelming opposition of the conservative press.

The conservative press is hardly limited to the Deep South or the farmlands. There are vast wastelands of liberal daily journalism in southern California, Chicago, Philadelphia and Detroit, where the metropolitan press dominates the cities while the conservative domain is extended by the large conservative chains like Copley and Gannett.

In that hotbed of journalistic radicalism New York City, all congressional districts support liberal-voting congressmen, but they don't have more than half the papers' support.

A psychojournalistic analysis of the Nixon-Agnew attacks on the media might show that important figures in the administration grew up on reactionary papers and never knew what a good newspaper was. The heartland of Nixonia is, of course, southern California. Today southern California is a study in right-wing journalism, with the *Los Angeles Times* rapidly leaving that tradition. But in the 1950s, when the Nixons and the Haldemanns and the Zeiglers and the Kleins were soaking up journalism, all of southern California was right-wing journalistic territory. Herbert Klein, Nixon's impresario of the media, was editor of the *San Diego Union,* a Copley property edited by retired military men for other retired military men. It is a case study in biased journalism. (It must have been sheer charm that led the Copleys, who publish in an area with significant numbers of Jews and Orientals, to take out a full-page advertisement in *Editor & Publisher* in 1968 celebrating "Jesus Christ, God's only begotten son.")

One reason most publishers have felt sullen under the Agnew attacks is that they believe he's right. They, too, think there is a radic-lib conspiracy among their reporters. The typical American newspaper publisher lives in agony knowing he is paying people to report political events he'd rather not see. In some places he asserts himself and there is no nonsense: the news is pure Republican party line. In most places the poor publisher feels restrained because he has a reporters' union, or there are powerful Democratic officeholders who might make business trouble for him. And there is the tradition of fairness that he doesn't want to be accused of violating, at least not in public. But when Agnew spoke, hundreds of publishers must have thought: "Spiro, I hear you talking."

The politics of the average American daily is an anachronism, meaningless to most of its readers. People buy newspapers for a variety of reasons, including the TV listings, pork chop prices and comic strips. But the American population is increasingly political and has growing sources of political information. Newspapers are prosperous today but so were the movies of 1939. At a time when publishers ought to be worrying about moving into the political and economic realities of the last half of the twentieth century, Nixon-Agnew are successfully nudging them deeper into the nineteenth.

Index

72 73 74 75 10 9 8 7 6 5 4 3 2